LECTURES ON
THE AMERICAN CIVIL WAR.

LECTURES

ON THE

AMERICAN CIVIL WAR

DELIVERED BEFORE THE UNIVERSITY
OF OXFORD IN EASTER AND
TRINITY TERMS 1912

BY

JAMES FORD RHODES, LL.D., D.Litt.

LECTURER ON THE HISTORY AND INSTITUTIONS OF THE UNITED STATES
OF AMERICA, 1912; AUTHOR OF THE HISTORY OF THE
UNITED STATES FROM THE COMPROMISE OF 1850
TO THE FINAL RESTORATION OF HOME RULE AT
THE SOUTH IN 1877; HISTORICAL ESSAYS

London

MACMILLAN AND CO., Limited

NEW YORK: THE MACMILLAN COMPANY

1913

Norwood Press
J. S. Cushing Co. — Berwick & Smith Co.
Norwood, Mass., U.S.A.

PREFACE

I READ these Lectures in the Schools before the University of Oxford during May 1912. They are printed as read with no very important exceptions. A few paragraphs and sentences as originally written were omitted in the reading to keep within the conventional fifty-five minutes; these are here restored. The account of Pickett's Charge in Lecture III has been expanded for the sake of greater clearness; likewise my story of Grant's Vicksburg campaign which, as read in Oxford, was excessively compressed.

The work of literary revision of the Lectures has been entrusted to my son, Daniel P. Rhodes, to whom, amongst other changes, I owe the rewriting of the Pickett Charge and the Vicksburg campaign.

Footnote references, in which only volume and page numbers are given, are to my History of the United States from the Compromise of 1850 to the Final Restoration of Home Rule at the South in 1877.

I have had the further benefit of a critical survey by David M. Matteson; to him I owe the plan of the map which shows the country at two different dates — an undertaking fraught with considerable difficulties. For the careful execution of the map I am indebted to George P. Brett.

The syllabus of the Lectures serves as a Table of Contents.

Boston, December, 1912.

CONTENTS

LECTURE I

ix

LECTURE II

LECTURE III

First response of the country to Proclamation of
Emancipation unfavorable. Policy completed by
Proclamation of January 1, 1863. Proclamation did
not excite servile insurrection. Lincoln pleaded for
gradual emancipation with compensation. McClellan
removed. Burnside met with a crushing defeat by
Lee. Depression of Lincoln. Loss of confidence in
him. Lee defeated Hooker, Burnside's successor in
command of the Army of the Potomac. Lee invaded
Pennsylvania. Meade succeeded Hooker. Defeated
Lee at Gettysburg. Grant took Vicksburg. England's attitude to the Civil War. Sympathy with the
North until Battle of Bull Run. William H. Russell's
letters to the *Times* swayed opinion in favor of the
North. Battle of Bull Run. Influence of the cotton
famine. Russell compelled to leave America. Seizure of Mason and Slidell. Jubilation at the North.
Sensation in England. Demand for the surrender of
Mason and Slidell. Demand complied with. Neglect
of England to detain war steamers *Florida* and *Alabama*. General belief in England that the North
could not conquer the South. Movement toward in-
terference. Gladstone's Newcastle speech, October 7,
1862. Decision that the existing policy of non-intervention should be continued. Sympathy of the common people with Lincoln's policy of emancipation.
Earl Russell's friendly neutrality in 1863. The case
of the iron clad rams at Birkenhead. Earl Russell
detained the rams. Grant a great general. Lincoln's
power. Grant in command of the Army of the Potomac. In his first campaign failed to crush Lee's army,
but his own was shattered. Gloom and dejection at
the North succeeded by joy at Farragut's and Sherman's victories. Lincoln reëlected President. Grant
forced Lee's surrender at Appomattox. Assassination
of Lincoln. Lee the representative of the Southern
cause. Lincoln necessary for the victory of the North.

LECTURES ON THE AMERICAN CIVIL WAR

LECTURE I

ANTECEDENTS OF THE AMERICAN CIVIL WAR
1850–1860

GARDINER'S title "History of Our Great Civil War" has always struck me as apt. A historian so careful in his use of adjectives could not have adopted one so expressive without reflection. The English Civil War was great in itself and its consequences, and, though it may not convey as important lessons to the whole civilized world as did that one of which Thucydides was the historian, yet for its influence on American colonial life and on the development of our history to the formation of our Constitution, it is for us a more pregnant study. Moreover Gardiner's history of it is a model for the historian of our Civil War.

There is risk in referring any historic event to a single cause. Lecky entitled his celebrated chapter, "Causes of the French Revolution." Social and political, as well as religious, reasons, according to Gardiner, brought on the Great Civil War.[1] Thucydides, on the other hand, though he did indeed set forth the "grounds of quarrel," stated his own belief that "the real though unavowed cause" of the war was "the growth of the Athenian power." And of the American Civil War it may safely be asserted that there was a single cause, slavery. In 1862 John Stuart Mill in *Fraser's Magazine*,[2] and Professor Cairnes in a pamphlet on the Slave Power, presented this view to the English public with force, but it is always difficult to get to the bottom of a foreign dispute, and it is not surprising that many failed to comprehend the real nature

[1] Gardiner's Great Civil War, I, 11.

[2] Dr. O. W. Holmes wrote to J. L. Motley, from Boston, March 8, 1862: "John Stuart Mill's article in *Fraser* has delighted people here more than anything for a good while. I suppose his readers to be the best class of Englishmen." Motley's Letters, II, 69.

of the conflict. When in July, 1862, William
E. Forster said in the House of Commons
that he believed it was generally acknowledged that slavery was the cause of the war,
he was answered with cries, "No, no!" and
"The tariff!"[1] Because the South was for
free trade and the North for a protective
tariff this was a natural retort, though proceeding from a misconception, as a reference
to the most acute tariff crisis in our history
will show.

In 1832, South Carolina, by act of her
Convention legally called, declared that
the tariff acts passed by Congress in 1828
and 1832 were "null, void, no law," and
that no duties enjoined by those acts
should be paid or permitted to be paid in
the State of South Carolina. It is a significant fact that she failed to induce any of
her sister Southern States to act with her.
By the firmness of President Jackson and
a conciliatory disposition on the part of the
high tariff party the act of nullification was

[1] IV, 80.

never put in force; [1] but the whole course
of the incident and the yielding of South
Carolina demonstrated that the American
Union could not be broken up by a tariff
dispute. Natural causes since 1832 have
modified the geographical character of the
controversy. The production of sugar in
Louisiana, the mining of coal and the man-
ufacture of iron in a number of Southern
States have caused their senators and representatives to listen kindly to pleas for a
protective tariff.

Here is a further illustration of the
unique character of the divisional or, as we
should say, sectional dispute concerning slavery. Sixteen years ago, the money question, the demand for the free coinage of
silver, took on a sectional character in ar-
raying the West and the South against the
East, but the advocates of the gold standard
always had a hearing and a party in the
States devoted to silver. But after 1850,
there was no antislavery party in the South

[1] I, 45.

and men advocating even the gradual abolition of slavery would not have been suffered
to speak.   Again, in 1896, natural causes
had play; they took from the dispute about
the money standard its sectional character.
The disappearance of the grasshoppers that
ate the wheat and maize, the breaking of the
severe drought of the preceding years, the
extension further west of the rain belt, good
crops of cotton, maize and wheat with a good
demand, brought prosperity to the farmers
and with it a belief that the gold standard
best served their interests.

Some of our younger writers, impressed
with the principle of nationality that prevailed in Europe during the last half of the
nineteenth century, have read into our conflict European conditions and asserted that
the South stood for disunion in her doctrine
of States' rights and that the war came because the North took up the gage of battle
to make of the United States a nation.   I
shall have occasion to show the potency of
the Union sentiment as an aid to the de-

struction of slavery, but when events are reduced to their last elements, it plainly appears that the doctrine of States' rights and secession was invoked by the South to save slavery, and by a natural antagonism, the North upheld the Union because the fight for its preservation was the first step toward the abolition of negro servitude. The question may be isolated by the incontrovertible statement that if the negro had never been brought to America, our Civil War could not have occurred.

The problem was a tougher one than had confronted Rome even if we regard as justified Mommsen's dire arraignment of slavery in his brilliant chapter. "Riches and misery," he wrote, "in close league drove the Italians out of Italy and filled the Peninsula partly with swarms of slaves, partly with awful silence."[1] In the South, the slaves belonged to an inferior race; the gulf is deep between the white race and the black. I wish, said James Madison, that

[1] I, 382.

I might work a miracle. I would make all the blacks white. I could then in a day abolish slavery.[1] Just before the war, a lunatic in an asylum near Boston, who took great interest in the different proposed compromises and solutions of the insoluble controversy, finally announced, I have found it! I know what will prevent the war. Countless pails of whitewash, innumerable brushes; make the negroes white!

I purpose devoting my first lecture to the antecedents of our Civil War and I shall begin the account with a statement of conditions in 1850. The issue of the war with Mexico gave the United States a large amount of new territory, known then as California and New Mexico, which under the Mexican law were free from slavery and ought to remain so unless this condition were removed by express enactment. But Calhoun, Senator from South Carolina, with ascendant influence over the Southern mind, had a theory to fit the occasion. He said

[1] I, 383.

that when the sovereignty of Mexico was succeeded by that of the United States, the American Constitution applied to the new territory, and as it recognized slavery, so it permitted slave owners to take their slaves into California and New Mexico; in other words it legalized slavery.[1] This new doctrine was eagerly embraced by the South. But the North, believing that slavery was wrong, demanded that the general government prohibit it in the new territory, and although the letter of the Constitution was silent on this subject, legislative precedent amply supported this demand as strictly constitutional. California for herself resolved the question. The discovery of gold promoted the settlement of this territory by a mass of seekers of fortune, many of them outcasts and vagrants, while others, though rough, hardy men, loving cards and drink, had a native sense of justice which demanded fair play. The speedy settlement of this hitherto unknown country

[1] I, 94.

led De Quincey to say, "She is going ahead at a rate that beats Sindbad and Gulliver";[1] and Bret Harte has feelingly portrayed the early settlers and their surroundings in "Tales of the Argonauts," "Luck of Roaring Camp" and "Outcasts of Poker Flat." The quasi-military government and the survival of the Mexican municipal authority did not prevent California from reaching the verge of anarchy and a majority were earnest that Congress should institute a stable territorial government, which it still failed to do because of the difference about slavery. Eventually the better class of immigrants, who were constantly increasing, took the lead in forming a State government. A Convention regularly chosen adopted a Constitution modelled after the constitutions of New York and Iowa and no objection whatever was made to the clause in the bill of rights, which forever prohibited slavery in the State. This was done from no moral motive, as men from the South, believing

[1] I, 113.

that slavery was right, joined with Northerners, who believed it wrong, in this prohibition, because they thought it would be
out of place in the new country.   As an old
mountaineer argued in a harangue to the
crowd, "In a country where every white
man made a slave of himself there was no
use in keeping niggers."[1]   Armed with her
excellent Constitution, California then proceeded in a regular manner to make a
natural and just demand.   In the parlance
of the day, she knocked at the doors of
Congress for admission into the Union, but
failed to receive a general welcome for the
sole reason that she had prohibited slavery.

As slavery was out of tune with the
nineteenth century, the States that held
fast to it played a losing game.   This
was evident from the greater increase of
population at the North.   When Washington became President (1789), the population
of the two sections was nearly equal, but
thirty-one years later, in a total of less

[1] I, 115.

than ten millions there was a difference of
667,000 in favor of the North, and when,
twelve years later still, the immigration
from Europe began, the preponderance of
the North continued to increase. The
South repelled immigrants for the reason
that freemen would not work with slaves.
In the House of Representatives, chosen
on the basis of numerical population, the
North, at each decennial census and appor-
tionment, gained largely on the South,
whose stronghold was the Senate. Each
State, irrespective of population, had two
senators, and since the formation of the
Constitution, States had been admitted in
pairs by a tacit agreement, each free State
being counterbalanced by a slave State.
The admission of California which would
disturb this equilibrium was resisted by the
South with a spirit of determination made
bitter by disappointment over California's
spontaneous act. The Mexican War had
been for the most part a Southern war;
the South, as Lowell made Hosea Biglow

say, was "after bigger pens to cram with slaves,"[1] and now she saw this magnificent domain of California escaping her clutches. She had other grievances which, from the point of view of a man of 1850 reverencing the letter of the Constitution, were undoubtedly well founded, but the whole dispute really hinged on the belief of the South that slavery was right and the belief of the majority of Northerners that it was wrong.

At the time of the formation of the Constitution the two sections were not greatly at variance. A large number of Southern men, among them their ablest and best leaders, thought slavery was a moral and political evil to be got rid of gradually. In due time, the foreign slave trade was prohibited, but the Yankee invention of the cotton-gin[2] made slavery apparently profitable in the culture of cotton on the virgin soil of the new States in the South; and Southern opinion changed. From being

[1] I, 87.   [2] I, 25.

regarded as an evil, slavery began to be
looked upon as the only possible condition
of the existence of the two races side by
side and by 1850 the feeling had grown
to be that slavery was "no evil, no scourge,
but a great religious, social and moral
blessing."[1] As modern society required
hewers of wood and drawers of water, the
slave system of the South, so the argument
ran, was superior to the industrial system of
England, France and the North.

In 1831, William Lloyd Garrison began
his crusade against slavery. In a weekly
journal, the *Liberator*, published in Boston,
he preached with fearless emphasis that
slavery was wrong and, though his immediate followers were never many, he set
people to thinking about the question,[2] so
that six years later Daniel Webster, one of
our greatest statesmen with a remarkable
power of expression, said, the subject of
slavery " has not only attracted attention

[1] Webster's Seventh of March Speech, Works, V, 338.
[2] I, 53.

as a question of politics, but it has struck a far deeper-toned chord. It has arrested the religious feeling of the country; it has taken strong hold on the consciences of men."[1] In the nineteen years before 1850 the opinion constantly gained ground at the North that slavery was an evil and that its existence at the South was a blot on the national honor.

In 1850, there were at the South 347,000 slaveholders out of a white population of six millions, but the head and centre of the oligarchy was to be found amongst the large planters, possessors of fifty or more slaves, whose elegance, luxury and hospitality are recited in tales of travellers, over whose estates and lives the light of romance and poetry has been profusely shed; of these, there were less than eight thousand.[2] Around them clustered the fashionable circles of the cities, composed of merchants, doctors and lawyers, a society seen to the best advantage in New Or-

[1] I, 72.   [2] I, 346.

leans, Charleston and Richmond. The
men composing this oligarchy were high-
spirited gentlemen, with a keen sense of
honor showing itself in hatred of political
corruption, resentment of personal attack
by speech or by pen, to the length of the
fatal duel and a reverence for and readiness
to protect female virtue. Most of them
were well educated and had a taste for
reading; but they avoided American literature as emanating mostly from New England, the hotbed of abolitionism, and pre-
ferred the earlier English literature to that
of the nineteenth century. But their ability
manifested itself not at all in letters or in
art, but ran entirely to law and politics, in
which they were really eminent. English
travellers before the Civil War liked the
Southerners for their aristocratic bearing
and enjoyed their conversation, which was
not redolent of trade and the dollar, like
much that they heard at the North.[1] It is
obvious that men of this stamp could not

[1] I, 347, 359, 361; VII, 172.

be otherwise than irritated when Northern speeches, books and newspapers were full of the charge that they were living in the daily practice of evil, that negro chattel slavery was cruel, unjust and barbaric. This irritation expressed itself in recrimination and insolent demands at the same time that it helped to bring them to the belief that property in negroes was as right and sacred as the ownership of horses and mules.

In 1850, the South repeatedly asserted that she must have her rights or she would secede from the Union; and her action eleven years later proved that this was not an idle threat. She would submit to the admission of California provided she received certain guarantees. There resulted the Compromise of 1850, proposed by Henry Clay and supported by Daniel Webster and finally enacted by Congress. [1] Under it California came in free. Slavery was not prohibited in New Mexico. Webster argued

[1] I, 122 *et seq.*

that such prohibition was unnecessary as the territory was not adapted to slavery. "I would not," he said, "take pains uselessly to reaffirm an ordinance of nature, nor to reënact the will of God."[1] The South obtained a more stringent Fugitive Slave Law. Most of the negroes yearned for freedom, and, while their notions of geography were vague, they knew that freedom lay in the direction of the north star, and with that guidance a thousand escaped yearly into the free States. The rendition of fugitive slaves was a right under the Constitution, and as the South maintained that the law of 1793 was inadequate, she demanded one more stringent. In the end, a bill based on the draft of James Mason (the Mason of Mason-Slidell fame) was enacted. It ran counter to the Roman maxim that, if a question arose about the civil status of a person, he was presumed to be free until proved to be a slave, thus laying the burden of proof on

[1] I, 147.

c

the master and giving the benefit of the
doubt to the weaker party. Under this
Act of ours the negro had no chance : the
meshes of the law were artfully contrived
to aid the master and entrap the alleged
slave. By an extraordinary provision, the
commissioner who determined the matter
received a fee of ten dollars if he adjudged
the negro to slavery and one half of that
amount if he held the fugitive to be a
freeman.[1] The real purpose of the law
was not so much to recover the runaway
negroes as it was to irritate the North (or,
in the current figure of speech, to crack the
whip over the heads of Northern men) by
its rigorous enforcement. To this end being
admirably designed, it became one of the
minor influences that brought the North
to her final resolute stand against the extension of slavery.

Mason was the sort of man to think that
he had done a clever thing when, in draw-
ing an act to enforce the constitutional

[1] I, 185.

right of the South, he made its enforcement needlessly irritating to the North. But it proved a menace and a plague to the section it was intended to benefit. For the Fugitive Slave Law inspired Harriet Beecher Stowe to write Uncle Tom's Cabin, the greatest of American novels which, in the interest that it aroused and the influence that it exerted, has not unfitly been compared to La nouvelle Héloïse. Though the author possessed none of Rousseau's force and grace of style, her novel, and the play founded on it, could not have secured the attention of England and France unless its human element had been powerfully presented. Macaulay wrote that " on the whole, it is the most valuable addition that America has made to English literature." [1] England and her colonies bought a million and a half copies. Two London theatres produced the play. Three daily newspapers in Paris published it as a serial and the Parisians filled two theatres nightly

[1] Trevelyan, II, 271.

to laugh at Topsy and weep at the hard fate of Uncle Tom.[1] Many other stories were written to exhibit the wrongs of the negro under chattel slavery, but they are all forgotten. Slavery, in the destruction of which Uncle Tom's Cabin had a potent influence, is gone, but the novel, published in 1852, is still read and the drama acted, telling the present generation of the great political and social revolution wrought in their father's time.

From 1852 to 1860, the year in which Lincoln was elected President, the influence of this story on Northern thought was immense. The author had made no effort to suppress the good side of slavery, but had shown an intelligent sympathy for the well-meaning masters, who had been reared under the system; at the same time she had laid bare the injustice, cruelty and horror of the white man's ownership of the negro with a fidelity to nature that affected every reader. The election of Lincoln is a great

[1] I, 284 *et ante.*

fact in the destruction of slavery and, in gaining voters for him, Uncle Tom's Cabin was one of the effective influences. It made a strong appeal to women, and the mothers' opinion was a potent educator during these eight years; boys who had read Uncle Tom's Cabin in their early teens reached the voting age at a time when they could give slavery a hard knock.[1]

The Compromise of 1850 was an adroit device, as compromises go, and, with the exception of the indefensible portions of the Fugitive Slave Law, was fair to both sections. It abated the antislavery agitation at the North and the threats of disunion at the South and would probably have maintained quiet between the two sections for a considerable period had not an able Democratic senator opened the question afresh in 1854.

Slavery, as a sectional issue, had first claimed the attention of Congress in 1820 in the form of a proposition to admit Mis-

[1] I, 285.

souri as a slave State. "This momentous question," wrote Jefferson from his retirement, "like a fire-bell in the night awakened and filled me with terror. I considered it at once as the knell of the Union."[1] The result of the agitation was the Missouri Compromise. Missouri was admitted as a slave State, but her Southern boundary of 36° 30' was henceforward taken as the line between slavery and freedom in the rest of the great territory of the Louisiana Purchase. North of that line slavery was forever prohibited.[2]

In 1854, Stephen A. Douglas, a senator from Illinois, filled the public eye. Though he had never received any systematic education, he was a man of natural parts and had achieved a considerable success at the bar; then, finding politics more to his liking than the law, he had been able so to commend himself to his community that his political advancement was rapid and, up to a point, practically continuous. He had become one of the leaders of the Democratic

[1] I, 39.   [2] I, 36.

party and craved the presidency; being no believer in the maxim that everything comes to him who waits, he naturally adopted the boldest methods for gratifying his restless ambition. As chairman of the Committee on Territories and leader of the Democrats in the Senate, he introduced a bill for the organization of the territories of Nebraska and Kansas, one clause in which provided for the repeal of the Missouri Compromise of 1820. Here was an open bid for Southern support in his contest for the presidency. His bill became a law and the slavery question was opened anew. For instead of being closed to slavery by formal Congressional act, these territories were now open to settlers from both North and South, the one bringing their horses and mules, and the others having the privilege of bringing their slaves as well.[1]

The North was indignant at this violation of a solemn compact by a movement initiated by one of her own sons. As I look back

[1] I, 425.

upon this episode, with every disposition to be fair to Douglas and not unmindful of apologies for his conduct that conscientious historical students have made, I believe that he merits strong condemnation from history. By his act was revived a perilous dispute that was thought to have been settled. Douglas loved his country and reverenced the Constitution, but he could not see the evil of slavery; he did not appreciate that it was out of tune with his century. Not intending, at first, to go the full length of repealing the Missouri Compromise, he found that, upon opening the question, he had invoked a sentiment at the South that demanded full measure.[1] To retreat would be cowardly, even ridiculous. He must go forward or give up his position as a leader. Therefore he demanded, in the end without evasion, the repeal of the Missouri Compromise and supported his measure by adroit but specious reasoning.

[1] Chadwick (Hart's American Nation, Causes of the Civil War, 58) thinks that Douglas yielded to an unconscious pressure.

He stood for the doctrine which went by the high-sounding name of popular sovereignty and meant that the people of the territories themselves should determine whether slavery should be protected or prohibited within their borders, and he accordingly carried the notion of local government to an unworkable and dangerous extreme, considering that the question involved was slavery. Give the people a chance to decide, he argued continually. " If they wish slavery, they have a right to it." " I care not whether slavery is voted down or voted up." [1]

Of parliamentarians, in the English sense of the word, Douglas is one of the cleverest in our annals. The conduct of his measure through the Senate, where he was opposed by men of remarkable ability and where the closure does not obtain, was a master stroke of parliamentary management. With the help of the President and the zeal of South-

[1] I. 447 ; II. 285. So far as I know, this last statement was not made until 1857, but it fits his argument of 1854.

ern representatives, who were quick to see their advantage, the House adopted Douglas's measure despite the rise of indignant sentiment in the North at the betrayal of a sacred pledge. This outburst of public opinion was predicted on the day that the Senate passed the bill. On that sombre March morning of 1854, when the cannon from the navy-yard was booming out the legislative victory, Senator Chase, an earnest opponent of the bill, said to his intimate and sympathizing friend, Senator Sumner, as they walked away from the Capitol together, " They celebrate a present victory but the echoes they awake will never rest until slavery itself shall die." [1]

Chase was right. The antislavery men, a powerful majority of the North, deemed the bill an outrage. From the press and the public platform, from the " stump," as we say, in grove or park, came emphatic condemnation of the conduct of Douglas and of the act of Congress. Douglas's un-

[1] I, 476.

popularity in the North was intense and widespread. It was then a common practice to burn in effigy the public man whose course was disapproved. "I could travel," said Douglas, "from Boston to Chicago by the light of my own effigies." [1] Arriving in Chicago, his home, he gave notice that he would address his constituents, but his opponents went to the meeting and, by cries of execration, denied him a hearing.

Like Mason's Fugitive Slave Bill Douglas's repeal of the Missouri Compromise reacted to the detriment of its author. It destroyed his chance for the presidency. It brought about the formation of the Republican party. On the 1st of January, 1854, the two chief parties in the country were the Democratic and Whig, the Democratic having the presidency and a good majority in both the Senate and the House. There was a third party, the Free-Soil, which, holding as its cardinal doctrine, opposition

[1] I, 496.

to slavery, sometimes held the balance of power in closely contested Northern States, but which had only a small representation in Congress. The repeal of the Missouri Compromise roused the dormant antislavery feeling in the country and brought home to many the conviction that a new party should be formed to unite Whigs, antislavery Democrats and Free-Soilers in their resistance to the aggression of the slave power. Seward's ability and political experience seemed to mark him out for leadership, but he was a devoted Whig and, as the Northern Whigs had, to a man, opposed the repeal of the Missouri Compromise and would form the predominant element in the new partnership, he thought that all antislavery men should enlist under their banner. Westerners thought differently and, being less trammelled by political organizations than their Eastern cousins, proceeded to inaugurate the movement that was really demanded by the posture of affairs. Five weeks after the repeal of the Missouri Compromise, a

large body of earnest, intelligent and rep-
utable men, the leading citizens of the
State of Michigan, came together at Jackson and, as the largest hall was inadequate
for their accommodation, they met in a grove
of famous oaks in the outskirts of the village. Here they resolved to suspend all
differences regarding economic or adminis-
trative policy, to act cordially and faithfully
in unison with all opposed to the extension
of slavery and to be known as Republicans
until the end of the contest.[1]   Other States
followed this example.

The year 1854 was one of political and
moral excitement. Though undoubtedly
the original impulse came from the repeal
of the Missouri Compromise, all the ensuing
agitation did not turn on the question of
slavery. The temperance question entered
into politics; more conspicuous than this
was the so-called Know-nothing movement,
the object of which was a political proscrip-
tion of foreigners, especially Roman Catho-

[1] II, 48.

lics.[1] Important as were their acts for
a twelvemonth or so, the Know-nothings
need not divert us from the main issue
which, as we study it in the elections of
members for the House of Representatives
in the autumn of 1854, was the repeal of
the Missouri Compromise — Should it be
upheld or denounced? In this contest the
Northern press had a marked influence and,
in its warm advocacy of the cause of freedom, wrote for itself a noble chapter. The
foremost journalist of the day was Horace
Greeley, who exerted his peculiar influence
through the *New York Weekly Tribune*,
which was estimated to have half a million
readers, many of whom looked upon it as a
kind of political bible. The revolution in
public sentiment was strikingly disclosed in
the elections of 1854. In the House, which
had repealed the Missouri Compromise, the
Democrats had been in a majority of 84;
in the succeeding one, they were in a minor-
ity of 75. Of forty-two Northern Demo-

[1] II, 50.

crats who had voted for the Repeal only
seven were reëlected.[1] While the North
deemed the Repeal an outrage, the South
hailed it with joy.[2] Believing that slavery
was right and that negroes were property,
she thought that an equal privilege in the
territory now in question was her due.
Douglas in his bill separated the vast territory into two parts, the northern part
Nebraska, the southern Kansas. The
South regarded this provision as indicating
an intention to give her a new slave State
in Kansas while Nebraska was entitled to
freedom. But under the Douglas scheme
of popular sovereignty the people of the
territory should themselves decide whether
or not they would have slavery. The
actual result was a contest between the
South and the North on the plains of Kansas.[3] The adjoining slave State, Missouri,
sent thither a number of settlers who, for
the most part, wished merely to better their
condition; and, at the same time, in

[1] II, 67.   [2] I, 496.   [3] II, 78 *et seq.*

response to the pioneering spirit of the age,
a large emigration from the Western free
States took place. Behind these natural
movements were an organized effort in
Missouri to make Kansas a slave State and
an Emigrant Aid Company in New England, whose purpose was to make her free.
At the first election for a territorial legislature, a mob of five thousand Missourians,
armed to the teeth, marched into Kansas,
took possession of the ballot-boxes and
chose the proslavery candidates, who, on
their meeting, legalized slavery, and, to
maintain it, adopted a code of laws of
exceptional harshness and severity. Meanwhile New England emigrants reënforced the
original Northern settlers until there was a
respectable free-state party wisely led.
These repudiated the territorial legislature
as illegal, organized at once a state government and applied to Congress for admission
into the Union, so that there existed in Kansas at the same time two governments and
two sets of people directly hostile to each

other. The President and the Senate supported the proslavery party, while the majority of the House, elected during the indignant protest against Douglas's Repeal of the Missouri Compromise, were on the side of the free-state settlers.

The cause of Kansas was declared to be the cause of the South and appeals were made for emigrants and for slaves. One of the Missouri leaders said, "If we can get two thousand slaves actually lodged in Kansas, our success is certain." But all the negroes were wanted in the cotton States for the production of cotton. Moreover, there was a lack of means in the South properly to equip and arm the young hardy men who were desired for the conflict. The most significant result of the appeals by the press and political leaders was the arming and equipment of two hundred eighty men raised in three of the cotton States, known from its leader as Buford's battalion, who after a blessing from the Methodist pastor and a promise of bibles from the Baptist, left Montgomery for Kansas to fight for the cause of slavery. At about the same time a meeting was held in a New Haven church to collect money for a company of seventy-nine emigrants who should go to Kansas to battle for freedom. A number of ministers and several of the Yale College faculty were present. Fifty Sharpe's rifles were wanted. Professor Silliman subscribed for one, the pastor of the church for a second, and, as the subscription went on, Henry Ward Beecher, a celebrated pulpit orator, said that if twenty-five were promised, his Plymouth Church would give the rest.[1] Henceforward the favorite arms of the Northern emigrants, Sharpe's rifles, were known as "Beecher's bibles." The men who bore them were called in the cotton States "Hireling emigrants, poured in to extinguish this new hope of the South"; at the North the Missouri invaders were called "border ruffians," whilst their allies, Buford's battalion, were scarcely in better odor. When feelings ran

[1] II, 153.

so high in the peaceful portions of the country, it is little wonder that Kansas itself was
soon in a state of civil war.   At first the so-
called "border ruffians" were the offenders,
but when a free-state company under the
leadership of John Brown had in one night
on the Pottawatomie deliberately and
cruelly murdered five proslavery men, it
could no longer be said that the work of
violence was all on one side. Guerilla
bands of both parties wandered over the
territory and engaged one another at sight.
No frugal settler of either party was safe
from pillage at the hands of marauders from
the other camp.   Women and children fled
the territory. Men slept on their arms.
Highway robbery and rapine prevailed over
all the country-side; "the smoke of burning dwellings darkened the atmosphere."[1]
As the proslavery faction had the Federal
government on its side, it claimed to be the
party of law and order and in that name
were committed its depredations, whilst the

[1] II, 216.

other faction killed and robbed in the name
of liberty. Yet, in a balancing of acts and
character, the free-state adherents of 1856
are superior to the proslavery partisans in
everything that goes to make up industrious
and law-abiding citizens. The free-state
men lost the larger amount of property and
the destruction caused by the proslavery
faction was much the greater.

Kansas was engrossing the attention of
Congress when there took place in the Senate an incident that profoundly affected
Northern sentiment. Charles Sumner, Senator from Massachusetts, had spoken on
"The Crime against Kansas," making use
of much exaggeration and turgid rhetoric in
his invective against the operations of the
slave power. It was not this portion of his
speech, however, that was responsible for
its unfortunate sequel, but a bitter personal
attack, with insulting allusions, on Butler,
a Southern aristocrat and Senator from
South Carolina. Two days later, after the
adjournment of the Senate, while Sumner

was sitting at his desk writing letters, he
was approached by Preston Brooks, a representative from South Carolina, who declared
that he had libelled South Carolina and his
relative, Senator Butler.   When he had
spoken, Brooks raised his cane and struck
Sumner on the head with all his might, con-
tinuing to strike until he had stunned and
blinded his victim.   The cane broke; even
then he rained blows with the butt on
the defenceless head.   Sumner instinctively
wrenched the desk from its fastenings, stood
up, and with wildly directed efforts attempted to defend himself.   Brooks struck
him again and again.   At last Sumner, reel-
ing, staggering backwards and sidewards,
fell to the floor, bleeding profusely and
covered with his blood.[1]

Sumner had an iron constitution and excellent health, but his spinal column was
affected so that he must spend the next
three and a half years in search of a cure.
He received medical treatment in Washing-

[1] II, 139, 140.   The assault was on May 22, 1856.

ton, Boston, London and Paris, but never regained his former physical vigor. By an almost unanimous vote of the Massachusetts Legislature he was reëlected to the Senate where his empty seat was eloquent for his cause. Not until December, 1859, was he able to resume and steadily pursue his senatorial career.

The assault struck the North with horror and indignation, while in the slave States it was approved by the press and by the people. The assailant was spoken of as the courageous and noble Brooks; indeed the South rallied to him as the champion of their cause.[1]

As the Senate was democratic and the House republican, Congress failed to agree on a bill that would dispose of the Kansas trouble. The contest in the legislative chambers was then transferred to the country and the opportunity for a verdict from the people was at hand, inasmuch as a President and a House of Representatives was to be chosen in this year of 1856. The Democrats

[1] II, 143, 147.

nominated Buchanan in preference to Douglas, because Buchanan had been out of the country as minister to England during these years and was not associated with the repeal of the Missouri Compromise and the consequent disturbance in Kansas. The Republican National Convention was an exceptionally earnest and patriotic body of men, yet it made an unfortunate nomination for President in Colonel Frémont, who lacked both the ability and the character demanded of the leader of so righteous a cause. But the Convention registered the popular will. It was a boon that he failed of election, as he was unfit to cope with the secession of the Southern States, which would certainly have ensued. The Republican declaration of principles was an improvement on the candidate. It demanded the admission of Kansas as a free State and declared it to be both the right and duty of Congress to prohibit slavery in the territories.[1]   The Re-

[1] The territories were organized divisions of the country under the control of the Federal government not admitted to the rights of statehood. See map.

publicans made an enthusiastic canvass, condemning the repeal of the Missouri Compromise and pointing to "bleeding Kansas" as its result. But Buchanan was elected President, and the Democrats regained control of the House of Representatives. As they still had the Senate by a majority of 12, they were in full possession of the executive and legislative branches of the government.[1]

Our government is singular in its complete separation of the executive, legislative and judicial powers. Under any polity, as Mr. Bryce observed,[2] we must come to the people at last; yet each branch of our government emanates from the people in a different manner. Districts of a population of 93,000 (I am speaking of 1856; our congressional districts are now much larger[3]) elect the members of the House of Representatives. The voters of each State choose a legislature which elects two senators.

[1] II, 169 *et seq.*   [2] American Commonwealth, II, 217.
[3] Under the census of 1910, 211,877.

The President is chosen through a method of indirect election, by the people of the United States, and he appoints the justices of the Supreme Court, who, however, must be confirmed by the Senate and who have a life tenure.

For three years the national legislature and executive had endeavored to solve the slavery problem with conspicuous failure. Now the Supreme Court was to try its hand. Its Chief Justice has great power in directing the consideration of the Court to constitutional questions which may arise in any case before it. The present Chief, Taney, had been on the Bench for twenty-two years and had gained a solid reputation for accurate knowledge of law and clearness of statement. Being of broadly patriotic temper, he made up his mind that his Court could settle the slavery question, and, in a case where it was necessary only to determine whether a certain negro named Dred Scott was slave or freeman, he delivered a carefully prepared opinion in which he as-

serted that "the right of property in a slave
is distinctly and expressly affirmed in the
Constitution"; that Congress had no more
power over slave property than over property
of any other kind; consequently the Missouri Compromise Act "is not warranted by
the Constitution and is therefore void."
Five judges agreed with Taney and these
made two-thirds of the Court. This decision
which neutralized the Republican doctrine
that Congress had the power to prohibit
slavery in the territories, was a blow to
those Republican leaders who were good
lawyers and who reverenced the Supreme
Court. It was met in the common-sense
way by Abraham Lincoln, who declared that
the Republicans offered no resistance to the
decision, but, believing it to be erroneous,
would do their best to get the Court to
overrule it as it had previously overruled
other decisions.[1]

This so-called Dred Scott opinion was
delivered two days after the inauguration of

[1] II, 251 *et seq.*

Buchanan, and though it did not dispose of the Kansas question, it gave a theoretical basis to slavery in the territories and furnished a strong support for the next move of the slave power.

The effort to make Kansas an actual slave territory had failed, as it had now within its borders only 200 or 300 slaves; but, as there were sixteen free to fifteen slave States, the proslavery party eagerly desired the political power of another State — its two senators and one or more representatives — to restore the equilibrium existing before 1850. A plan to this end was promptly devised. Originating probably with Southerners of high position in Washington, it found ready instruments in Kansas. A sham election resulted in a constitutional convention, which framed a Constitution establishing slavery in the most unequivocal terms and which, as it could not avoid the time-honored precedent of submitting the Constitution to a popular vote, provided for a submission of it that,

in the words of the Democratic governor of
the territory, was "a vile fraud, a base
counterfeit and a wretched device" to prevent the people from deciding whether or
not they would have slavery.   For the
Convention did not dare to provide for a
fair election, as the proslavery advocates
would have been outvoted three to one.
President Buchanan, though from a Northern State, had a great admiration for Southern politicians whose persuasion and threats
induced him to support this plan, which was
known as the Lecompton scheme.[1]

The proceeding was a travesty of the doctrine of popular sovereignty, and when the
Senate met in December, 1857, Douglas
boldly denounced it.[2]   His manner was
haughty and defiant as he set himself in
opposition to his party, the Democratic,
which was strongly entrenched in all three
branches of the government, and he did not
hesitate to characterize the scheme "as a
trick, a fraud upon the rights of the people."

[1] II, 276 *et seq.*   [2] II, 283.

Despite Douglas's opposition, the Democratic Senate voted to admit Kansas as a State under her proslavery constitution, but to this the House, in closer contact with the people, would not agree. The excitement in Washington was intense, and, during a heated all-night session of the House, an altercation between a Southern and Northern representative resulted in a fisticuff, in which thirty men were engaged, but no weapons drawn. In the end, a compromise was agreed upon between the Senate and the House, the effect of which was to offer to Kansas a large amount of public lands if she would accept the Lecompton constitution. By a vote of 11,300 to 1800 she rejected the bribe and thus determined that slavery should not exist in Kansas. But the affair left an irreconcilable breach in the Democratic party.[1]

We are now in the year 1858, in the spring of which year Douglas was the best-known and most popular man in the North,

[1] II, 301 *et ante.*

so effectively had he won back public esteem by his resistance to the Lecompton project. The relations between him and the Republicans in Congress were cordial and the possibility that their party should nominate him as their candidate for the presidency two years hence was considered by no means out of the question. Seward was coquetting with him but had no idea of stepping aside in his favor if the conditions were propitious for Republican success. Douglas must stand this year for reëlection as senator from Illinois and the leading Eastern Republicans, nearly every Republican senator and many representatives desired that their party should make no opposition to him. Greeley in his powerful journal warmly favored his return to the Senate; but the Republicans in Illinois, under the lead of Abraham Lincoln, protested against it.

The son of a shiftless poor white of the slave State of Kentucky, Lincoln was brought up in that State and the southern part of Indiana, moving to Illinois when he was twenty-one. The southern Indiana of that day might have suggested the Eden of Martin Chuzzlewit. Its farms and villages were rude and ill-kept; fever and ague were unrepressed; the most ordinary refinements of human existence were lacking even to what would be considered there to-day the actual necessaries of civilization. Lincoln said that the story of his early life was told in a single sentence of Gray's Elegy,—

" The short and simple annals of the poor."

His schooling was necessarily meagre, but he had an active mind and an extraordinary power of application. He was a thorough student of the Bible and Shakespeare and mastered the first six books of Euclid. Reading few books, he thought long and carefully on what he read, and his opinions on all subjects were generally the result of severe study and profound reflection. He studied law and at the age of twenty-eight began practice; but his interest in politics was so deep as to brook no enduring rival. He loved and believed in the common people; he amused them and interested them in himself. His early associates were American born, dwellers in village and lonely farm and the stories he told them were of the order that there prevails; if they were amusing, he cared little if they were coarse as well. A frequenter of the tavern he used neither spirits nor tobacco; his personal morals were good. He served one term in the Illinois legislature, another in the United States House of Representatives, but not belonging to the dominant party in his State, he failed to remain continuously in the public service. He reached a high rank in his profession, being esteemed the strongest jury lawyer in Illinois; but he was a bad advocate in an unjust cause. The repeal of the Missouri Compromise diverted his attention from law to politics, and a speech, in which he demolished Douglas's political and historical sophistry, made him the leader of the Republicans in his State. Lincoln was then nearly elected United States senator, but although deeply disappointed, he, with rare magnanimity and judgment, withdrew in favor of another candidate, to prevent the defeat of the cause. Intensely ambitious, he nevertheless loved truth and justice better than political place and power. At twenty-four he had been dubbed "honest Abe." At no time in his eventful life did he do anything to cast a shadow of discredit on this epithet sprung from the rude soil of Illinois.[1]

At the age of forty-nine, Lincoln was hardly known beyond the confines of his own State or, wherever known in the East, was regarded as a "backwoods lawyer"; yet he stood forth to contest the senatorship with the most formidable debater in the country. He gave the keynote of the campaign in the most carefully prepared speech that he had ever made, addressed to the Republican State Convention, which had unanimously nominated him as the candi-

[1] II, 313 *et ante.*

E

date of their party for senator. "'A house divided against itself cannot stand,'" he said. "I believe this government cannot endure permanently half slave and half free. . . . Either the opponents of slavery will arrest the further spread of it and place it where the public mind shall rest in the belief that it is in the course of ultimate extinction; or its advocates will push it forward till it shall become alike lawful in all the States, old as well as new, North as well as South."[1]

When Douglas went to Chicago to open the campaign, his town gave him an enthusiastic reception, which contrasted strikingly with his home-coming four years earlier. In his first speech he attacked with great force Lincoln's "House-divided-against-itself" doctrine, which doctrine, though soon to be demonstrated in hard and cruel fact, had in 1858 not many adherents. When submitted to a dozen of Lincoln's political friends before public pronouncement, it had received the approval of only one, and after

[1] II, 314.

it was uttered, there was no doubt whatever that, inasmuch as it was in advance of his party's thought, it counted against him in his contest with Douglas. Douglas's progress through his State amounted to a continuous ovation. Travelling in special trains — an unusual proceeding at the time — the trains being drawn by decorated locomotives, he was met at each city by committees of escort, and, to the thunder of cannon and the music of brass bands, was driven under triumphal arches, on which was emblazoned the legend, "Popular Sovereignty." The blare and flare of the campaign were entirely to his liking, but they were merely the theatrical accessories of a truly remarkable actor.

His short and massive frame was surmounted by an enormous head, from which shone forth eyes of a penetrating keenness; his appearance alone justified the title of "little giant" long since given him. A melodious voice and a clear incisive enunciation combined with apt and forcible gestures to point the ingenious arguments that kindled a genuine enthusiasm in the sons of Illinois, whose admiration and love he had gained.

As a boy, I saw Douglas often at the house of my father, who was his warm personal and political friend. His great head seemed out of proportion to his short body, giving one the idea of a preponderance of the intellect. But he was not a reader and I do not remember ever seeing a book in his hand. Knowing little of Europe, he had absorbed the history of his own country and used this knowledge with ready skill. His winning manner was decisive with boys and he gained a hold on young voters, which he retained until Lincoln came to appeal to their moral sense.

Lincoln realized that the current was setting against him, but he felt no regret for his action in setting forth the positive doctrine of his opening speech. Believing that his adroit and plausible opponent could be better answered from a platform shared in common, he challenged him to a series of joint debates. He showed a profound confidence in his cause when he pitted himself against the man who in senatorial debate had got the better of Seward and Sumner and more recently had discomfited the champions of the Lecompton scheme. Lincoln was tall, gaunt, awkward; his face was dark, yellow, wrinkled and dry, voice shrill and unpleasant, movements shy and odd. In oratorical power and personal magnetism he was inferior to Douglas, but when he was warmed to his subject, his face glowed with the earnestness of conviction and he spoke with excellent result.

The joint debates, in different portions of the State, were seven; they are the most celebrated in our history. Illinois, though by no means fully aware of the crucial character of this contest, was nevertheless sufficiently aroused to turn out audiences of from five to twenty thousand at these day meetings, held in groves or on the prairie. Here Lincoln by his remorseless logic brought

Douglas to bay. He showed that the slavery question was at rest when Douglas disturbed it by the Repeal of the Missouri Compromise. *Why could you not leave it alone?* he asked with emphasis. The doctrine of Popular Sovereignty was "*a living creeping lie.*" Douglas, he asserted, has undertaken to " build up a system of policy upon the basis of caring nothing about *the very thing that everybody does care the most about.*" The real issue, Lincoln truly declared, is whether slavery is right or wrong.

Each partisan who went to these meetings thought that his candidate got the better of the other. Douglas won the senatorship and for the moment the general opinion of the country that he had overpowered his antagonist in debate; but when the debates were published in book form, in 1860, opinion changed. Careful reading showed that in the dialectic contest Lincoln prevailed over Douglas; but he had an immense advantage in the just cause and the one to which public sentiment was tending.[1]

The country now had four leaders, Lincoln, Douglas, Seward and Jefferson Davis. In October, 1858, Seward declared that there existed " an irrepressible conflict" between slavery and freedom.[2] During the ensuing session of the Senate, Davis took the position that Congress was bound to protect slavery in the territories. This was a startling advance on the doctrine of Calhoun and the Supreme Court, who had simply maintained that Congress had no right or power to prohibit it. In truth the apparent necessity of fostering slavery had driven the Southerners to extreme ground. Having failed to secure Kansas or any other Western territory, they now made an effort to acquire Cuba, where the slave system already prevailed. Further acquisitions were hoped for in Mexico and Central America, where it was believed that slavery could be easily introduced. Moreover, as

[1] II, 339 *et ante.*   [2] II, 344, 347.

there were not negroes enough to cultivate
the cotton, sugar and rice in the existing
slave States, a large, possibly a predominant,
party began to advocate the revival of the
African slave trade. Indeed, during 1859,
a large number of negroes were smuggled
into the Southern States.[1]

Towards the end of 1859, John Brown
made his memorable attack on slavery. The
method of the Republicans did not suit him;
they respected slavery in the States where
already established. The Abolitionists had
" milk-and-water principles," issuing merely
in talk. His own belief was that action was
needed. Gathering eighteen followers, five
of whom were negroes, he succeeded, on
the cold, dark Sunday night of October 16,
in capturing the United States armory, ar-
senal and rifle works at Harper's Ferry,
Virginia, which were under civil, not military, guard. He expected the slaves of Virginia and the free negroes of the North to
flock to his standard. These he would arm

[1] II, 369; Chadwick, Causes of the Civil War, 18, 62.

with pikes. Fortified against attack and subsisting on the enemy, he would make his name a terror throughout the South, so that property in man would become insecure and eventually slavery might thus be destroyed. When his friends urged the folly of attacking the State of Virginia, the United States government and the slave power with so small a band, he said, " If God be for us, who can be against us?" Imbued as he was with the lessons of the Old Testament, he undoubtedly imagined God would work for him the wonders that He had wrought for Joshua and Gideon.

The attempt, of course, failed quickly. During the Monday fighting was carried on with the people of Harper's Ferry; early next morning Colonel Robert E. Lee, at the head of a company of United States Marines, took Brown and four of his followers prisoners. Ten of them had been killed.[1] Of the inhabitants and attacking parties five were killed and nine wounded.

[1] Four had escaped.

Virginia was in an uproar. While the rabble would have liked to lynch Brown, men of education and position could not but admire his courage. He had a fair trial, was of course found guilty and, forty-five days later, hanged.

The Southerners believed that he had "whetted knives of butchery for their mothers, sisters, daughters and babes." To Northern statesmen, it was clear that he could have achieved success only by stirring up a servile war and unchaining passions such as had made the memory of San Domingo horrible. If this were the whole of his strange story, History could visit on Brown only the severest condemnation. But his words and behavior between arrest and execution, his composure on the scaffold under circumstances peculiarly distressing must give the ingenuous student pause. Though the contemporary raptures of Emerson and Victor Hugo [1] now look preposter-

---

[1] Emerson said, "I wish we might have health enough to know virtue when we see it and not cry with the fools 'madman' when

ous, it must nevertheless be admitted that Brown suffered martyrdom for the anti-slavery cause. Nor is it possible to forget how Northern soldiers, as they marched to the front to fight for the freedom of the negro, were inspired by the stirring music and words, —

"John Brown's body lies a-mouldering in the grave,
But his soul goes marching on." [1]

Three days after the execution of Brown the Thirty-sixth Congress assembled. In the intense excitement that prevailed the House attempted organization in the usual manner by election of a Speaker, but this

a hero passes"; and he further spoke of Brown as "that new saint, than whom none purer or more brave was ever led by love of men into conflict and death—the new saint awaiting his martyrdom, and who, if he shall suffer, will make the gallows glorious like the cross." The citation is from a lecture delivered Nov. 8, 1859. Brown was hanged Dec. 2.

Victor Hugo wrote: "In killing Brown, the Southern States have committed a crime which will take its place among the calamities of history. The rupture of the Union will fatally follow the assassination of Brown. As to John Brown, he was an apostle and a hero. The gibbet has only increased his glory and made him a martyr." Hugo suggested this epitaph for him: "Pro Christo sicut Christus." II, 413, 414.

[1] II, 383, *et seq.;* Villard's John Brown, 426 *et seq.*

was soon found to be difficult, as no one of
the four parties who met in the chamber
had a majority, although the Republican
was the most numerous. The contest began
on December 5 and did not end until February 1, when a conservative Republican was
elected. At times some of the Southern
members became excited and made extravagant statements. They accused the Republicans of complicity in John Brown's
raid; they censured Seward for his "irrepressible conflict" speech; and they threatened to dissolve the Union in the event of
the election of a Republican President. On
one day an altercation between two Illinois
members, on another a hot personal dispute
between a Southerner and Northerner, end-
ing in a challenge to personal combat,[1] helped
to keep the excitement up to fever heat. A
few days later an anti-Lecompton Democrat
from New York was making bitter personal
remarks about another member when a
pistol accidentally fell to the floor from the

---

[1] Grow, the Northerner, made a dignified refusal.

breast pocket of his coat. Some members thinking that he had intentionally drawn the weapon rushed towards him ready for a fight if one should ensue. A senator from South Carolina wrote in a private letter, " I believe every man in both Houses is armed with a revolver — some with two — and a bowie knife."[1] Jefferson Davis, feeling the responsibility of leadership, was generally guarded in the expression of his views, but he gave the Senate to understand that the Union would be dissolved if Seward was elected President.

We are now in the year 1860, a year for the election of a President. As arranged four years previously, the Democratic Convention met in Charleston, South Carolina, the hotbed of disunion. The Douglas dele-

[1] II, 424 *et ante.* "Mr. Grow (a prominent Republican representative) told the writer in 1895, that, during the period just before the War, every member intended as much to take his revolver as his hat when he went to the Capitol. For some time a New Englander, who had formerly been a clergyman, was the only exception. There was much quiet jesting in the House when it became known that he, too, had purchased a pistol." Frederic Bancroft, Life of W. H. Seward, I, 503.

gates were in a majority and adopted their platform, whereupon the delegates from the cotton States seceded from the Convention. As under the Democratic rule, it required two-thirds to nominate a President, and as Douglas could not secure that number, the Convention adjourned to meet in Baltimore forty-six days later. There Douglas was finally nominated, but as soon as this nomination seemed inevitable, another secession took place and these seceding delegates, joined by most of those from the Charleston Convention, adopted the Southern platform and nominated a Southern Democrat.

In the meantime the most interesting of our Conventions, and the first one to resemble a huge mass-meeting, was held in Chicago. The 466 Republican delegates met in a wigwam, a temporary frame structure, which, it was said, would hold ten thousand people, although three times that number of strangers, mostly from the Northwest, clamored for admittance. The conditions for serious deliberation were unfavorable, yet the delegates acted as wisely as if they had assembled in a hall fit for conference with ample leisure and a suitable environment. In their platform they asserted that the rights of the States should be maintained inviolate; denounced the John Brown invasion " as among the gravest of crimes"; inveighed against the new dogma that the Constitution of its own force carries slavery into the territories; denied " the authority of Congress, of a territorial legislature or of any individual to give legal existence to slavery in any territory"; and branded " the recent reopening of the African slave-trade as a burning shame to our country and age." [1] There were only two possible nominees for President, Seward and Lincoln. Seward had wrought in the vineyard longer, was considered the more radical of the two and partly for this reason the weaker candidate in four of the so-called doubtful States. Lincoln had attracted much atten-

[1] II, 464.

tion by his debates with Douglas and by a noble speech made in February in New York City. He received the nomination on the third ballot.[1]

Our presidential election is made by States, each State choosing the same number of electors as she has senators and representatives in Congress. Lincoln carried all of the free States except New Jersey, whose electoral vote was divided between him and Douglas; having thus a majority of the electoral votes, he was regularly chosen for the presidency and would enter into office on the following 4th of March.[2]

In the election of Lincoln the North had spoken. In every man's mind rose unbidden the question, What would be the answer of the South?

[1] II, 470 *et ante.*　　　　[2] II, 500.

LECTURE II

FROM LINCOLN'S ELECTION, 1860, TO HIS PROCLAMATION OF EMANCIPATION, 1862

THROUGH the election of Lincoln the majority of the Northern people declared that slavery was wrong and should not be extended. The sectional character of the contest is clearly manifest, inasmuch as in ten out of the eleven States that afterwards seceded and made up the Southern Confederacy Lincoln did not receive a single vote. As soon as the result was known, South Carolina led off with a prompt reply. Since 1850, disunion sentiment within her borders had been strong, but a considerable opposition had always existed. Now, the day after Lincoln's election,[1] the majority suddenly expanded to unanimity. The crowd that thronged the streets of Charleston felt that they had an undoubted griev-

[1] Nov. 6, 1860.

ance and that their sole remedy was secession. The legislature immediately called a
convention, an act that was received with
enthusiasm. Speeches, newspaper leaders,
sermons from the pulpit were alike in their
absolute sincerity. The North has made an
attack on slavery, our cherished institution
— so ran the unanimous contention — it has
encroached upon our rights. We can preserve our liberty and our property only by
separation. "The tea has been thrown
overboard, the revolution of 1860 has been
initiated." It is a striking evidence of the
misunderstanding between the two sections
that, while eleven-twelfths of the Northern
voters thought the South had lorded it over
the North since the annexation of Texas,
South Carolinians, almost to a man, and a
majority in the cotton States, were equally
convinced that they had suffered grievous
wrongs at the hands of the North. A phi-
losopher, living in the South but sympathizing with the North, recalled a remark of
Thucydides as applying to the present

situation : " The Greeks did not understand each other any longer, though they spoke the same language ; words received a different meaning in different parts."[1]   No South Carolinian would have asserted that any overt act of oppression had yet been committed, but all would have said that a free people must strike at the first motion of tyranny.   It soon became apparent that the course on which the State was entering with such enthusiasm involved a great sacrifice. Business went from bad to worse, merchants found it difficult or even impossible to pay their debts and the banks of Charleston were forced to suspend specie payments.   Plantation slaves could be sold for only half what they would have brought before the election of Lincoln.   In Charleston the value of all kinds of property except cotton fell fifty per cent.   Nevertheless the people showed no sign of faltering.   There was a round of meetings, pole raisings, dedications of ban-

[1] Francis Lieber, II, 489.   Lieber quoted from memory and gave a free translation.   See Jowett, III, 82.

ners, fireworks and illuminations; and the music of this nascent revolution was the Marseillaise. The delegates who composed the Convention were, for the most part, men of distinction, whose silver hairs were a check to rash and impulsive action, yet, after certain methodical preliminaries, they speedily adopted the ordinance of secession by a unanimous vote. The proclamation that the State of South Carolina was an independent commonwealth renewed the enthusiasm which was manifested by cries of exultation and shouts of gladness and the other usual phenomena of popular rejoicing.[1]

In the meantime, Congress met and the country looked to it to resolve the difficulty. It has been asserted that if our government had been carried on by a responsible ministry like that of England, some expedient would have been devised to prevent war; but, as a matter of fact, we have always been ready in time of emergency to borrow

[1] III, 114–125, 192–206.

the adaptable political machinery of any government by discussion. The Senate Committee of thirteen, which framed the Compromise Measures of 1850, resembled a coalition ministry and now a Senate Committee of the same number was appointed to consider "the grievances between the slaveholding and the non-slaveholding States" and to suggest, if possible, a remedy, which committee calls to mind the "Ministry of all the Talents." The constitution of the Committee was eminently fair, each party and section being suitably represented. In ability, character and influence all the senators stood high; three of them, Davis, Seward and Douglas, were leaders of public sentiment. There was reason to believe that if the Union could be saved by act of congress, these senators would discover the way. The aim of compromisers generally was to prevent the six cotton States from following South Carolina in acts of secession and to keep the border slave States in the Union. The people of the North for the

most part had some idea of the peril in
which the Union stood and they believed
that in these thirteen men lay the best hope
of an acceptable compromise. It was indeed a rare committee. No two men in public life stood for sentiments so diametrically
opposed as Seward and Jefferson Davis, yet
they were on friendly social terms and had
at one time been intimate. The incessant
and bitter factional strife of seven years
could not sour the genial nature of Douglas,
who was prepared to extend the right hand
of fellowship to every man on the committee with the possible exception of Davis.
In addition to a willingness to sink any
personal animosities, he also stood ready to
yield somewhat of his political views in
order to preserve the Union.

The Committee of "all the Talents"
went to work diligently and with the sincere
purpose of preventing further secessions.
The pivot on which a settlement turned
was the Crittenden Compromise, known
from the name of its author, a senator and

member of the Committee. Amongst its many provisions, the really important one, involving the main point at issue, concerned the status of the territories. It was provided that an amendment to the Constitution should reëstablish the old line of the Missouri Compromise, the parallel of 36° 30', as the boundary between slavery and freedom; south of this line slavery should be protected, north of it prohibited. This provision, though entirely satisfactory to both the Northern Democratic and the border State senators, was by no means acceptable to the cotton States, unless it should be expressly provided or understood that the protection to slavery should apply to any territory subsequently acquired south of the compromise line.[1]

The pressure of business interests at the North for the preservation of the Union was strong. The depression in trade, the feverish and panicky condition of the New York stock market, the suspension of specie pay-

[1] III, 146 *et seq.*

ments by the banks of Charleston, Washington, Baltimore and Philadelphia, the apprehended repudiation of debts due the North by Southern merchants, the payment by the government of interest at the rate of twelve per cent per annum for a small loan, — all these developments were bound to incline Republican senators toward some compromise which should check the secession movement.[1] Especially was this the case of Seward, senator from New York and in touch with the great city's financial interests, leader of the Republican party in Congress and a confirmed opportunist in politics. He never pronounced in favor of the Crittenden Compromise, nor on the other hand did he condemn it.[2] He wavered, and if he could have secured the support of Lincoln, would undoubtedly have given it his countenance. The influence of the two would have carried it in Committee and secured its adoption by Congress, pre-

[1] III, 171, 251.
[2] III, 156 *et seq.*; Bancroft, Life of Seward, II, 32–34.

venting further secessions and for the moment avoiding the war.

It may seem curious to Englishmen that in a pure democracy like ours, so long an interval should elapse between the election and the inauguration of a President. The election of 1860 was a political revolution, yet not until four months after Lincoln was chosen did he assume the reins of office. In the interim, he exercised a large influence, but it was wholly indirect and in the form of counsel given in private conversation or personal letter to senators, representatives and other important men. He well understood the needs of the situation and, having offered Seward the position of Secretary of State, the leading post in his Cabinet, he was able through him and others to dictate the policy of his party. On every point but one, Lincoln was willing to compromise; on the question of the extension of slavery he was inflexible. If we yield there, he wrote, the South has us under again. "All our labor is lost and sooner or later must be done over. The tug has to come now, and better now than later." He saw clearly that if the line of latitude of 36° 30' should be drawn between slavery and freedom, filibustering would recommence and through this and other means, the South would seek to acquire Cuba, Mexico and Central America in order to augment the slave power and put us again "on the high road to a slave empire."[1]

The Republicans therefore defeated the Crittenden Compromise in committee;[2] they then came forward with a proposition unacceptable to the cotton States. On December 28, 1860, the Committee adopted a resolution that they "had not been able to agree upon any general plan of adjustment,"[3] and thus gave virtual notice to the country that the cotton States could not be retained in the Union. But this inference that separation must follow, though obvious enough to the historical student of to-day, was by no

[1] III, 160, 161, 269.
[2] III, 154, 167; Chadwick, Causes of the Civil War, 172–181.
[3] III, 175, 178.

means generally drawn at the time. Crittenden and Douglas, nowise despairing, tried to
further the original plan of settlement by
placing it on a new basis. They proposed
the submission of the Crittenden Compromise to a popular vote, having a well-
grounded confidence that a large majority
of the country would favor it. Had the
referendum been as popular then as it is
now, they might have persuaded Congress
to adopt this proposal, but the Republican
senators, obviously fearing the result, never
permitted it to come to a vote in the Senate.[1] The House of Representatives tried
its hand at compromise, but failed to agree
upon any practicable measure. On the in-
vitation of Virginia, the largest and most
important border slave State, a Peace Convention, made up of notables from twenty-
one States, assembled in Washington and
threshing " the straw of debate anew "[2]

[1] III, 253, 262.
[2] III, 306. James Russell Lowell's comment was: "The usual
panacea of palaver was tried; Congress did its best to add to the
general confusion of thought; and, as if that were not enough, a

adopted a plan of adjustment, which, carried as it was by a narrow margin of votes, had no force at the back of it and resulted in nothing.[1]

The Civil War in England, wrote Gardiner, "was rendered inevitable" because "a reconciliation between opposing moral and social forces" could not be effected.[2] Here is an exact statement of our own case in 1861. The Civil War might have been averted had the North yielded to the South and in the words of Lincoln ceased references to "slavery as in any way a wrong" and regarded it "as one of the common matters of property" speaking "of negroes as we do of our horses and cattle."[3] In other words, the North must repress its own enlightened sentiment regarding slavery and ignore that of England, France, Germany

convention of notables was called simultaneously to thresh the straw of debate anew and to convince thoughtful persons that men do not grow wiser as they grow older."

[1] III, 305.

[2] History of the Great Civil War, I, 1.

[3] II, 332.

and Italy.   Or, on the other hand, the war
might have been prevented had the Southerners had a change of heart, reverted to
the sentiment of the founders of the republic that slavery was an evil and agreed to
limit its extension.   The logical result would
have been gradual abolition and the North
stood ready to bear her share in compensat-
ing the owners of slaves.   But anybody who
should have promulgated such a doctrine in
the South in 1861 would have been laughed
at, hooted or mobbed.[1]

Secession moved apace.   The conventions
of the six cotton States in quick succession
passed ordinances dissolving their bonds
with the Federal Union.   The movement
was of the people, and not dictated by a
dozen or a hundred conspirators, sending
forth decrees from their secret conclaves in
Washington.   Legislatures called conventions of the people.   After animated can-
vasses in Alabama, Georgia and Louisiana,
and a full understanding of the matter in all

[1] III, 269; Chadwick, Causes of the Civil War, 56.

of the States, the question in the popular elections of delegates to the conventions was really put: Shall it be immediate secession, or delay with the endeavor to secure our rights within the Union? and the answer was always, "Immediate secession." This action was justified in accordance with two doctrines which had been maintained side by side by Calhoun, the great leader of the South after the fathers of the Republic, — the rightfulness of slavery and the sovereignty of the States. The Southerners saw in the election of Lincoln a reproach that they were living in the daily practice of a heinous wrong, and rather than submit to the meddling of unfriendly hands with their sacred institution, they invoked the remedy of secession which they deemed their undoubted right, because the Constitution was a compact to which the States were parties in their sovereign capacity; and they bolstered up this policy with the assertion that the North had violated that Constitution by opposing the extension of slavery, thus denying them their rights in the common territories.[1]

Most Europeans are struck with the strangeness of the doctrine of secession; that, in its organic act, the nation should in effect have provided for its own dissolution, by permitting the withdrawal of a component part or parts, on the ground of grievances, of whose validity the aggrieved should be the sole judge. Here was no claim of the common right of revolution. The cotton States did not maintain that revolution was justified, but that in the delegation of powers to the Federal government, the right of withdrawal from the Union was reserved; this right they now exercised. In 1861, it was an open question in the United States whether the Constitution was indeed such a compact. The North, influenced by the teaching of Webster, denied the right of secession; the South, swayed by Calhoun, asserted it. An impartial judge must have realized that there were two sides to the

[1] III, 273.

dispute ; and after hearing the historical and traditional arguments, he might have found a decision difficult. But nothing is clearer than that the right of secession would never have been invoked save for the protection of slavery.[1]

From the point of view of political expediency secession was thoroughly unwise. The election of Lincoln did not carry with it a Republican Congress ; opposed to him was a majority of the Senate and the House of Representatives ; and every justice of the United States Supreme Court except one leaned against his policy. Under the Dred Scott decision of this Court, the Southerners possessed the right of taking their slaves into the territories. In this whole controversy nobody spoke more to the point than Charles Francis Adams when he termed the alleged grievances of the South "mere abstractions." And if the counsel of their wisest leaders could have prevailed, the Southern States would have been less pre-

[1] III, 119 *et seq.*, 203, 280.

cipitate. Prepare yourselves for a long and bloody war, was the burden of Jefferson Davis's speeches to his followers in the course of his progress from Washington to the capital of his State.[1] Very different this from the boast — which was common enough — that the North was so absorbed in money getting that she would not fight, or, if she did, that one Southerner could "whip four Yankees."

The ardor and confidence of the people soon reacted upon the leaders themselves. Delegates of seven cotton States assembled in Montgomery to form a Southern Confederacy. They elected Jefferson Davis, the ablest statesman of the South, their President and adopted a permanent Constitution with few essential departures from the Constitution of the United States ; three of these departures concerned negro slavery. In the Confederate Constitution the right of property in negro slaves was expressly stated ; the obligation to recognize and pro-

[1] III, 297 *et seq.*

G

tect slavery in any new territory that might be acquired was finally and explicitly imposed on the Congress ; and, in the different provisions relating to the cherished institution the words "slave" and "slavery" stood forth in bold veracity, contrasting sharply with the ingenious circumlocution of the Federal Constitution in which the use of these words had been studiously avoided.   In deference to the opinion of Christendom the foreign slave-trade was prohibited.   The preamble of the Constitution affirmed in effect the right of secession and called attention to the religious character of the people by " invoking the favor and guidance of Almighty God." [1]

By way of propitiating England and securing, if possible, her active assistance, it was sometimes asserted at the South that one cause of the secession was the protective tariff, which was alleged to have been forced upon the South by the North.   And some color was given to this assertion by a section

[1] III, 291, 320.

of the Confederate Constitution which forbade the imposition of duties on foreign imports to foster any branch of industry. It was difficult during the war to persuade many Englishmen that the tariff was not at the bottom of the dispute, although in truth it was a very unimportant issue. When Lincoln was elected, the tariff of 1857 — a revenue tariff of something less than twenty per cent — was in operation and while the Morrill tariff bill, increasing the duties, had passed the House, it could not have passed the Senate except for the secession of the seven cotton States and the consequent withdrawal of fourteen senators. If the cotton States had stipulated for a continuance of the tariff of 1857 as a necessary condition of their remaining in the Union, this demand would have been joyfully acceded to ; and their approval of this tariff law is shown by its enactment by the Confederate Congress at its first session.[1]

[1] III, 58, 204, 294, 315, 322; John Sherman's Recollections, I, 187.

In the once proud Union there were now two established governments. The Southerners in Montgomery had proceeded in an orderly manner and made it evident that they shared with the North her political aptitude. Both peoples were God-fearing, professed the same religion, spoke the same language, read the same literature, revered the same Constitution, had similar laws and with the one notable exception the same institutions. The difference was frankly stated by the Vice-President of the Southern Confederacy, Alexander H. Stephens, who said: The foundations of our new government are laid; " its corner-stone rests upon the great truth that the negro is not equal to the white man; that slavery is his natural and normal condition. . . . This stone [the doctrine that negro slavery is right] which was rejected by the first builders [the fathers of the republic] ' is become the chief of the corner ' — the real ' corner-stone ' in our new edifice." [1]

Evident though it be that slavery was the cause of the secession, the ingenuous and the thoughtful (calling to mind that Plato believed slavery necessary and Aristotle deemed it " both expedient and right ") must withhold their censure from the slaveholders. No American can forget that Washington and Robert E. Lee, two of the noblest products of our life, were owners of slaves. Again, if we of the North will but ask ourselves what would have happened if our Pilgrim and Puritan ancestors had settled in Virginia instead of in Massachusetts and we had ourselves inherited slaves, it is hardly possible to answer otherwise than that most of us would have fought for slavery.

The system of slavery becomes so interwoven with the political, economic and social life of the community that to remove it is to endanger the whole fabric. Willingly to renounce it would be little short of heroic; to cling to it is become second nature. If "Cæsar was the entire and perfect man," and if slavery in Rome was a most arrant sin and abomination, desolating "God's fair world," as Mommsen wrote, how difficult was this evil to grapple with may be realized when we find our historian constrained thus to apologize for his hero: "Cæsar could not abolish slavery." [1] Add, then, a difference in race and color between the master and the slave and the problem becomes harder still.

Sympathy rather than censure is the due of the American slaveholders. The evil left its mark upon the Southern gentleman, but so lightly as hardly to tarnish his character, for he relegated the repulsive part of slavery to unscrupulous hirelings, the overseers and slave-traders. Impetuous and domineering, quick to anger, mainly indifferent to scientific truth, and no worshipper of progress, the Southern gentleman belonged more to the eighteenth than the nineteenth century. [2] It is regrettable that these slaveholders, and the lawyers, merchants and doctors who united with them

[1] Mommsen, IV, 546, 593, 621.   [2] I, 359 et seq.

to make up the society of the South, did not in 1861 follow the counsel of their wiser leaders and seek redress in the Union,[1] for slavery was safer in it than out of it, as was foreshadowed at the time and as the result proved. But passion got the better of reason and again shaped the course of a great people.

Now that the Southern Confederacy regarded itself as established by the regular procedure in Montgomery, the North had to choose between peaceable separation and war. Shortly after Lincoln's election, Greeley had forcibly advocated in the *New York Tribune* the policy of letting the cotton States go in peace [2] and this proposal received at different times considerable support in the North. If a body of water as wide as the English Channel had separated the seven cotton States from the rest of the Union, such would have been the solution,

[1] III, 210.

[2] As General Scott expressed it " Wayward sisters depart in peace."   III, 341.

but, no considerable natural barrier existing, Lincoln was fully justified in saying in his inaugural address, "Physically speaking we cannot separate." On the other hand, the idea of preserving the Union by force was regarded with abhorrence by the two heroes of the war Abraham Lincoln and Robert E. Lee. "The ugly point," said Lincoln, "is the necessity of keeping the government together by force, as ours should be a government of fraternity."[1] "A union," wrote Lee, "that can only be maintained by swords and bayonets, and in which strife and civil war are to take the place of brotherly love and kindness, has no charm for me."[2]

The North showed its disposition to prevent disunion by carrying through Congress by the necessary two-thirds vote an amendment to the Constitution guaranteeing slavery indefinitely in the States;[3] in other words the institution would have been protected where it already existed. This

---

[1] III, 160, 317.   [2] Long, Life of Lee, 88.   [3] III, 313.

Amendment, which would have received the necessary ratification by the States had not the war ensued, was numbered the Thirteenth and the mistake that the South made is emphasized by the contrast with this and our actual Thirteenth Amendment, adopted four years later which abolished slavery forever.[1]

On March 4, 1861 Lincoln was peacefully inaugurated in Washington. He delivered an address that was moderate but firm and to the point, announcing that he had no purpose of interfering with slavery in the States, denying the right of secession and declaring that he would enforce the law in all the States, using his power to hold "the property and places belonging to the government, and to collect the duties and imposts." This last declaration irritated the South, as she was determined to resist by force any such action on the part of the President.[2] The only question now was when and where

[1] V, 50.   [2] III, 316.

the war would begin; and it seemed almost certain that Fort Sumter in Charleston Harbor with its garrison of United States troops would furnish the occasion for the first clash. The surrender of this fort had been demanded by South Carolina and later by the Southern Confederacy. Lincoln seemingly confronted with the alternative policy of surrender or reënforcement of the garrison, decided on neither, but as provisions were running short, he adopted the plan of sending supplies. South Carolina was notified of this decision by the President himself; Montgomery, by South Carolina. The result was a demand for the evacuation of Fort Sumter, refusal, bombardment, artillery duel between Sumter and the Confederate batteries lasting thirty-four hours and, in the end, surrender.[1]

April 12, 1861 is the notable day of the commencement of our Civil War by the firing of the Confederate guns upon the United States flag. At the time when

[1] III, 337, 346 *et seq.*

Lincoln decided on sending provisions to Fort Sumter, both he and Davis had undoubtedly come to believe that war was inevitable and each was anxious to avoid striking the first blow because of its probable effect on public sentiment at the North. Davis had good reason to regret that matters so fell out that the South became the aggressor, while Lincoln might well be grateful for the blunder that gave him in his time of trouble a united North. Still praying and hoping that actual hostilities might be averted, the people of the North were profoundly moved when they realized that civil war had begun. The shots fired at Sumter convinced everybody that the time for argument and compromise, of discussion and entreaty had passed; that the dispute was not to be settled by Congress or by conventions, or at the ballot-box and that this peace-loving people must suspend their industrial activities and prepare for the stress of war. When the President called for 75,000 militia to suppress combinations obstructing the execution of the laws in seven of the Southern States, they gave their approval as with a single voice and rose almost as one man to his support. In this uprising of the people, their blood was stirred as it had not been stirred since the Union was formed. Militia regiments and military companies which had been organized merely for the purpose of exercise, for social intercourse or for Fourth-of-July parades, hastened to prepare themselves for actual fighting. Men who had never dreamed of a soldier's life were now eager to enlist. Working-men, mechanics, clerks, students and professors of the colleges, many sons of wealthy and influential families enrolled themselves at once for the common cause. Men of position in civil life went out as officers of companies and regiments, but when such places were lacking they shouldered muskets and served in the ranks. Individuals, towns, cities and States offered money freely. Patriotism spoke from the pulpit,

the platform, the stump and with the
voice of the press. "The attack on Fort
Sumter," wrote Emerson, "crystallized the
North into a unit." The feeling that the
South had been precipitate and unreason-
able and that she was clearly in the
wrong was almost universal. That she had
wickedly rebelled, had without just and
sufficient cause begun a civil war, well expressed the sentiment of those who, after
listening to passionate utterances at the
public meetings, went straightway to the
enlisting officer and enrolled themselves as
volunteers. The speakers declared that
the people must preserve the Union and
maintain the government; and this was
clearly the purpose in the minds of those
who enlisted during the first months of
the war. [1]

The people of the Confederate States
were elated over the bombardment and
evacuation of Fort Sumter. They regarded
Lincoln's call for troops as a declaration of

[1] III, 357.

war, forcing them to arm for the defence of their property and their liberties. Believing in the constitutional right of secession, they regarded his attempt to coerce them back into the Union as nothing less than a measure for their subjugation. The uprising of men and the proffers of money matched those which were forthcoming at the North. The best blood offered itself to fight for country and cherished rights.[1]

It has been said that the American Civil War was remarkable in that it was waged on account of a difference of constitutional interpretation. The support for this statement is that each side obscured the real reason why it submitted its cause to the God of Battles, the South maintaining that they fought for the sovereign rights of States, the North because they resisted the dissolution of the Union. Whether the ostensible or the real reason of the war be considered, there is something inspiring in the thought that these two peoples threw

[1] III, 381.

aside money-getting and sordid calculation and entered on a course of self-sacrifice for the sake of principle.

The firing on Fort Sumter and the President's call for troops decided at once the course of Virginia. Two days after Lincoln's proclamation, her convention passed an ordinance of secession, and, in recognition of the importance of her adhesion, her chief city, Richmond, was made the capital of the Southern Confederacy. Three other slave States quickly followed her example and became constituent parts of the new government.[1] Three of the border slave States, Maryland, Kentucky and Missouri were kept in the Union by good management, the chief measure of which was the executive skill and energy of Lincoln.[2]

The Union of twenty-three States and the Confederacy of eleven were now definitely arrayed against each other. Twenty-two million people confronted nine million, and of the nine million three and a half

[1] III, 383, 385, 396.   [2] III, 388 *et seq.*

million were slaves. The proportion was nearly that of five to two. The Union had much greater wealth, was a country of a complex civilization and boasted of its various industries; it combined the farm, the shop and the factory. The Confederacy was but a farm, dependent on Europe and on the North for everything but bread and meat, and before the war for much of these. The North had the money market and could borrow with greater ease than the South. It was the iron age. The North had done much to develop its wealth of iron, that potent aid of civilization, that necessity of war; the South had scarcely touched its own mineral resources. In nearly every Northern regiment were mechanics of all kinds and men of business training accustomed to method in their daily lives, while the Southern army was made up of gentlemen and poor whites, splendid fighters, of rare courage and striking devotion, but as a whole inferior in education and in a knowledge of the arts and appliances of modern life to the men of the North. The Union had the advantage of the regular army [1] and navy, of the flag and of the prestige and machinery of the national government; the ministers from foreign countries were accredited to the United States; the archives of what had been the common government were also in possession of the Union.

The Southern people, in their pursuit of independence, were by no means dismayed at the spectacle of the united North and the odds of number and wealth against them. Did not the Grecians, they asked, vanquish Xerxes, did Philip of Spain subdue Holland? Nevertheless, in making the effort to gain their independence, the Southern people had undertaken a stupendous task; they had started out on a road, the end of which was at best doubtful; they had gone to an extreme, before proceeding to which it would have been better to endure some-

[1] 17,000 men when Lincoln was inaugurated. Nicolay and Hay, IV, 65.

H

what of grievance. They said they were fighting for liberty, yet they must shoulder the burden of their own denial of liberty to three and a half million human beings. They had the distinction of being the only community of the Teutonic race which did not deem human slavery wrong; in their social theory, they had parted company with England, France, Germany and Italy, and were ranged with Spain and Brazil.

The aim of the Northern men was to save the Union, to maintain the integrity of the nation. They had undertaken to conquer the wills of five and one-half million people — a community as advanced as themselves, except, owing to their peculiar institution, in the arts and manufactures, in business training and in scientific thought, and apparently their superiors in certain qualities which go to make up the soldier. Moreover, the nature of the conflict required the Northern troops to take the offensive by marching into the Confederate States; the fighting must be on Southern soil. Not the defence of Washington but the taking of Richmond was the task before them. For such warfare, the ratio of five to two in population was none too great, and required to be supported by the actual superiority in wealth and in industrial resources. Had the disparity been less, the North might have failed, especially as the expectation of the South that, by an exchange of its cotton with Europe, it would be able to supply itself with the implements and munitions of war, and the necessaries of life seemed by no means extravagant.[1]

The preponderating asset of the North proved to be Lincoln. Himself one of the " plain people " he both represented and led them; between the day of the firing on Sumter and the 4th of July following, when he called Congress together in special session, he gained a clear conception of the nature of the contest and realized that he might carry it on successfully as long as he had the support of public sentiment. When

[1] III, 397 *et seq.*

he addressed Congress, he had also the people in mind and he appealed to them with lasting effect. He needed their support, as his proclamation, ordering a substantial increase of the army and navy,[1] and his authorization to the commanding general, in proper cases, according to his discretion, to suspend the privilege of the writ of habeas corpus were stretches of constitutional authority.[2] The minister from the Hanseatic towns to Washington, a shrewd observer withal, wrote that Lincoln exercised unlimited power, to as great an extent, if not even greater, than Louis Napoleon, the only difference being that the Emperor had the army and the President the people at his back.[3]

In purely political matters, Lincoln had not his equal in public life but this country

[1] 42,034 volunteers for three years; 22,714 for the regular army; 18,000 for the navy. III, 394.

[2] Congress indemnified him for his act in increasing the army and navy, but did not come to a vote on the habeas corpus matter. III, 438. See also Lincoln, Complete Works, II, 59; Nicolay and Hay, IV, 176.

[3] III, 442.

attorney of Illinois was now become commander-in-chief of the army and navy of
the United States; having received neither
practical military training nor theoretical
instruction he was suddenly called upon to
conduct a great war.   In this respect his
marked inferiority to Jefferson Davis was
striking.   Davis was a graduate from the
Military Academy of West Point, had
served brilliantly as colonel during the war
with Mexico and afterwards had for four
years made an efficient head of the United
States War Department.[1]

Lincoln, conscious of his deficiency, made
an unofficial offer of the active command of
the Union forces to Robert E. Lee, the
officer in the United States service who had
the most worthy record and gave the best
promise of capable leadership.   Lee declined
the offer for the reason that he could take
no part in an invasion of the Southern
States, resigned his commission, accepted
the generalship of the Virginia forces and

[1] I, 389.

eventually became commander of the army of Northern Virginia, the most important and the most celebrated army of the Southern Confederacy.[1]

If Lee had seen his duty in the same light as did two other well-known Virginia officers, Scott and Thomas, who steadfastly adhered to the Union, Lincoln would have had a right arm and the war would have been shorter. Lee was drawn in both ways. He had a soldier's devotion to the flag and loved the Union, which was especially dear to him as product of the labor of Washington; he deemed "slavery as an institution a moral and political evil." Although believing that Northern aggressions had given the South just cause of grievance he did not consider the grievance sufficiently acute for resort to revolution — and to him secession meant nothing less. Nevertheless when Virginia seceded, his notion of States' rights seconded by a strong feeling of allegiance to his State prevailed, after a painful struggle,

[1] III, 365, 380; IV, 29.

over all other considerations. A careful survey of his life and character is perfectly convincing as to the motives leading to this momentous decision; a high sense of honor pointed the way, a pure and inexorable conscience approving.

Lee, now fifty-four, showed in his face the ruddy glow of health whilst his head was as yet untinged with gray. Physically and morally he was a splendid example of manhood. Tracing his lineage far back in the mother-country and having in his veins the best of Virginian blood, he seemed to have inherited all the virtues of a chivalrous race without any of their vices. Honest, sincere, simple, magnanimous, forbearing, courteous and dignified, he was at the same time sensitive on points of honor but was generally successful in keeping a high temper under control. After his graduation from West Point, his life had been exclusively that of a soldier, yet he had none of a soldier's bad habits. He used neither spirits nor tobacco, indulged rarely in a social glass of wine, and cared nothing for the pleasures of the table. He was a good engineer and had won distinction in the war with Mexico. The work that was assigned him had been performed in a systematic manner and with conscientious care. " Duty is the sublimest word in our language," he wrote to his son. Sincerely religious, Providence was to him a verity and it may be truly said that he walked with God. Indeed in all essential characteristics, Lee resembled Washington and, had the great work of his life been crowned with success or had he chosen the winning side, the world would doubtless have acknowledged that Virginia could in a single century produce two men who were the embodiment of public and private virtue.[1]

Before composing the fine battle-pieces in his history of Frederick the Great, Carlyle wrote, " Battles ever since Homer's time, when they were Fighting Mobs, have mostly ceased to be worth reading of. . . .

[1] III, 411.

How many wearisome bloody Battles does
History strive to represent!"[1]   Although
the thoroughgoing history of a war must of
necessity be largely one of campaigns and
battles, it will be my aim in these lectures
to treat briefly of this phase of my subject
and to dwell on the salient characteristics
of the conflict and their bearing on its issue
rather than on the sequence of movements
of the armies engaged.

"Bull Run," the first battle, was precipi-
tated by the North in the hope of opening
a way for the capture of Richmond.   On a
hot July day (1861), a Union army, composed for the most part of green soldiers,
attacked an equal number of Confederates
likewise green.[2]   The first charge resulted
in the baptism of General Thomas J. Jackson, with a name that exactly suited his conduct on this occasion.   The Confederates

[1] French Revolution, Book VII, Chap. IV.

[2] In the Northern army were nearly 1600 regulars and three
Massachusetts regiments which since January had had somewhat
of drill.   In the Southern army were five South Carolina regiments and the Hampton Legion which had been under discipline
more than six months.   III, 444, 451.

were in full retreat and as they ran up the slope of a plateau they saw his brigade standing in line calmly awaiting the onset, an example and encouragement to the panic-stricken host, whose general cried out, "Look at Jackson! There he stands like a stone wall!"[1] As "Stonewall" Jackson he was known till the day of his death and ever afterwards.

The battle was eventually decided by a timely reënforcement at a critical moment of 2300 Confederates. The Union troops broke and ran. The volunteers' retreat became a rout and then a panic. "A confused mob entirely demoralized"[2] fled to the shelter of the fortifications near Washington.

The North, although amazed and bitterly disappointed at this reverse, was not long inactive. A second uprising took place. Under authority, previously given to the

[1] III, 447.

[2] McDowell, the general in command, telegraphed, "The larger part of the men are a confused mob entirely demoralized." III, 450.

President by Congress to accept the services of 500,000 volunteers, recruiting went on with vigor, and the time for which men engaged themselves was three years or during the war. In a week the North had recovered from its dejection, prepared for a long conflict. The South received her great victory with a quiet sense of triumph and expressions of profound gratitude to Jehovah, who had wrought so powerfully in her behalf. It was believed that the North, far from giving up the contest, would be spurred to redoubled efforts by the initial repulse.[1]

Because of some minor successes in Western Virginia, Lincoln and, in the main, the country, thought they had discovered an able general in McClellan, and he was forthwith placed in command of the troops around Washington, to whom he gave the designation of "Army of the Potomac." He was an excellent organizer and well versed in the theory of his profession. After he had

[1] III, 456.

been in command a little over a month
William H. Russell wrote to the *Times*,
"Never perhaps has a finer body of men in
all respects of *physique* been assembled by
any power in the world, and there is no
reason why their *morale* should not be im-
proved so as to equal that of the best troops
in Europe."[1] But McClellan was no fighter.
Nursing the delusion that the Confederate
force in front of him was equal to his own
he would not attack, although he really outnumbered them three to one. Russell, who
was a keen observer and had visited the
South — who had, moreover, witnessed the
rout at Bull Run — thought that McClellan
ought to beat the enemy "in spite of their
advantages of position."[2] But as Lowell expressed it, "Our chicken was no eagle after
all."[3] Anthony Trollope, who paid us a
visit at this time, wrote that "belief in Mc-
Clellan seemed to be slipping away."[4] But
the general continued to drill and organize
the troops, letting slip an extraordinary op-

[1] III, 493.   [2] III. 495.   [3] III, 499.   [4] III, 579.

portunity for striking a decisive blow. With the end of the year 1861, eight months and more of war had accomplished nothing towards bringing back into the Union a single Confederate State. On the contrary the shedding of blood had made the chasm wider.

In February 1862 hope came from the Southwest where Ulysses S. Grant won an important victory. Having invested Fort Donelson [1] he repulsed a sortie and forced the Confederate garrison to surrender, incidentally acquiring the name expressive of his resolute character. The Confederate general asked for terms. None but "Unconditional Surrender" was Grant's reply: U. S. being the initials of his name, he became known thenceforth as "Unconditional Surrender Grant."[2] The North rejoiced with exuberance if somewhat prematurely. "The underpinning of the rebellion seems to be knocked out from under it," wrote Chase.[3]

[1] In the State of Tennessee on the Cumberland River.
[2] III, 593.
[3] Secretary of the Treasury. III, 598.

When Doctor Oliver Wendell Holmes went into his lecture room at the Harvard Medical School, the class began clapping loudly, then cheering, until, in his own words, "I, a grave college professor, . . . had to give in myself, and flourishing my wand in the air, joined with the boys in their rousing hurrahs."[1]

The fall of Donelson was to the South what Bull Run had been to the North,[2] the first serious reverse and doubly bitter, for that matter, inasmuch as the inactivity of the Army of the Potomac following upon Bull Run itself had led the Confederates to believe that in the field they were invincible. During the period of dejection that ensued, the permanent government of the Confederacy was established and Davis was inaugurated President in Richmond for a term of six years.[3] On his recommendation, the Confederate Congress passed a conscrip-

[1] III, 598.

[2] In connection with the capture of Fort Henry on the Tennessee River ten days earlier. III, 582.

[3] The government of the Confederacy was carried on for one year under the provisional constitution and the legislative body

tion act requiring of all white men between the ages of eighteen and thirty-five three years of military service.[1] It was nearly a year later that the North was forced to adopt this rigorous but just method of carrying on a war.

Less than a month after Donelson, occurred the fight between the *Merrimac* and the *Monitor*, which attracted especial atten- in England as it was the first encounter between ironclads. The *Merrimac* had with the utmost ease destroyed two wooden vessels of war, and was preparing for further blows to be directed against the blockade of Southern ports — an indispensable condition of Northern success — when she was intercepted and engaged by the *Monitor*. The battle demonstrated that the *Merrimac* could be held in check : she did no further damage.[2]

was called the provisional Congress. Davis was President of the Confederacy under this temporary organization. The first Congress under the permanent Constitution met Feb. 18, 1862, four days previous to Davis's inauguration.   III, 322, 600.

[1] III, 606.   [2] III, 608 *et seq.*

The effective work of the Union navy was further seen in the taking of New Orleans, a city of 168,000 inhabitants, the chief commercial port and the largest city of the South. It was "the crowning stroke of adverse fortune" said the Confederate Secretary of War.[1] New Orleans was so well known in Europe as an important trading point that its capture had a profound effect on opinion in England and France.[2] Could these successes be followed up by others, the North might speedily triumph but it was soon to appear that Fate had decreed otherwise. When it seemed as if "that rare son of the tempest,"[3] a great commander, had appeared, Grant through carelessness, allowed his prestige to fade. Partially surprised at Shiloh, he converted a defeat into a drawn battle only by a timely reënforcement and with enormous loss. His record in the regular army, seven years before the civil war, had been clouded by habits of intemperance,

[1] Official Records Series IV, II, 281.   [2] III, 630.

[3] Parkman, Montcalm and Wolfe, I, 181.

which resulted in his resignation and a general impression that "his life was hopelessly wrecked."[1] Now it was feared that he had had a relapse and the pressure on the President for his removal was great. But Lincoln stood by Grant saying with great earnestness to one who had stated the general protest, *"I can't spare this man; he fights."*[2]

Of the Army of the Potomac, under the command of McClellan, Edward Dicey wrote, "I have seen the armies of most European countries and I have no hesitation in saying that, as far as the average raw material of the rank and file is concerned, the American army is the finest."[3] These men full of courage and eager for a speedy end to the war were longing to be led against the enemy but their general would not give the word. Had he seized the moment of discouragement of the Confederates over their reverses in the Southwest, a cheap victory awaited him. Before Donelson Lincoln, by the Constitu-

[1] III, 596.   [2] III, 627 *et ante.*   [3] III, 604.

I

tion the Commander-in-Chief, in great distress and realizing the necessity of action, said in his whimsical way, " If General McClellan does not want to use the army I would like to *borrow* it." [1]   From entreaty he passed to command and then the General haggled over the plan of campaign.   The President desired the advance to be made directly on Richmond while McClellan wished to transport his army part way by water and make the movement up the Peninsula.   At that time, no Northern general had developed sufficiently to warrant a change in commanders so Lincoln yielded the point and gave consent to McClellan's plan.[2]   But the general's procrastination had allowed the Confederates time to recover from their reverses so that, when he came in sight of the spires of Richmond, Joseph E. Johnston, the successful commander at Bull Run, had a well-equipped force of 63,000 to meet his 100,000.   Meanwhile Stonewall Jackson made a swift march northward,

[1] III, 580.   [2] III, 614; IV, 2 *et seq.*

won a series of brilliant battles, alarmed the President and Secretary of War for the safety of Washington and thus prevented a contemplated reënforcement of 40,000 troops to the Union army before Richmond.

Although McClellan had started on an offensive campaign, it was not he but his adversary who took the initiative. Johnston made the attack, brought on a battle of two days' duration and achieved a partial success although meeting in the end with a repulse. The Union troops pushed forward within four miles of Richmond but receiving no order from their commander to hold the ground, fell back to the lines occupied before the battle. Johnston was wounded and Robert E. Lee succeeded to the command of the Army of Northern Virginia. Reënforced by Stonewall Jackson, he brought on the " Seven Days' Battles" in the course of which his success was not continuous, for the Union army was a formidable fighting machine even though its Commander did not know how to use it. McClellan was forced to abandon his offensive attitude and retreat to the James River: his Peninsular campaign had been an utter failure. During that week of hard fighting, Lee gained the love and confidence of his soldiers, which were never afterwards lost but grew larger as the war went on.

Once again was it the turn of the North to be plunged in gloom, and far deeper this time than after Bull Run. Lowell wrote in a private letter, "I don't see how we are to be saved but by a miracle." [1] "I have managed to skim the newspaper" wrote Charles Darwin to Asa Gray, "but had not heart to read all the bloody details. Good God! What will the end be?" [2] Lincoln grew pale and haggard with anxiety and dejection. But he said, "I expect to maintain this contest until successful, or till I die or am conquered, or my term expires, or Congress or the country forsakes me." [3] He called for 300,000 more three years' men. He made

---

[1] Letters, I, 322. [2] More letters of C. Darwin, I, 203. [3] IV, 55.

up a new army and summoned a man from
the West[1] to command it; he ordered another general[2] to Washington as General-
in-Chief who proved too timid to exercise
his authority but became useful as the President's chief-of-staff. Throughout this interval of gloom and demand for further
self-sacrifice, Lincoln retained the confidence and support of the people. A favorite
song during this dreary summer was, "We
are coming, Father Abraham, three hundred
thousand more."[3]

McClellan and his army were withdrawn
from the Peninsula. The military records
show confusion and hopeless mismanage-
ment in the efforts of the three generals, the
President and his Secretary of War to work
together in harmony. On the other side
Lee was supreme; he consulted no one;
now he took to studying the new general
from the West. "Frederick the Great,"
wrote Carlyle, "always got to know his

---

[1] John Pope, IV, 97.   [2] Henry W. Halleck, IV, 97.
[3] IV, 55, 76, 97.

man after fighting him a month or two ; and took liberties with him or did not take accordingly."[1] This task of learning to comprehend one's adversary was made comparatively easy in our Civil War, for the reason that most of the opposing commanders had become personally acquainted at West Point or during their service in Mexico. The Western general issued a tactless and boastful address to his new army. In military attainments, he was inferior to McClellan and in temper his opposite, being an impetuous and incautious fighter. Lee and Jackson played with him, crushing and demoralizing his army and again causing considerable alarm lest Washington be taken.[2] In the shifting of troops, McClellan had

---

[1] IV, 116.

[2] IV, 97 *et seq.* Under date of Sept. 7, 1862, Charles Eliot Norton wrote to George W. Curtis : " These days . . . have been in some important respects the most disheartening that we have yet been through. They have been worse than days of more serious disaster, for they have betrayed alike the incompetence of our generals and the vacillations of our administration at a time when there was special need of good generalship and of vigorous purpose." *Atlantic Monthly*, November 1912, 607.

been deprived of all actual command. But now he was the only resource. The President was compelled to put him at the head of the combined armies.[1] Rank and file were overjoyed. They loved McClellan and greeted him now with rousing cheers which showed their eagerness to fight if he would lead.[2] Lee had crossed the Potomac river into Maryland and was for the first time encamped in full force on Northern soil. A lucky revelation of his immediate projects now supplied McClellan with a brilliant opportunity to crush the invading forces.[3] To maintain his line of communication, Lee was forced to divide his army. His written order

[1] Under date of Sept. 7, 1862, Welles, the Secretary of the Navy, made this note in his Diary:

"The President said with much emphasis: 'I must have McClellan to reorganize the army and bring it out of chaos . . . there is no remedy at present, McClellan has the army with him.' My convictions are with the President that McClellan and his generals are this day stronger than the Administration with a considerable portion of this Army of the Potomac. It is not so elsewhere with the soldiers, or in the country, where McClellan has lost favor. The people are disappointed in him, but his leading generals have contrived to strengthen him in the hearts of the soldiers in front of Washington." I, 113, 114.

[2] IV, 136.   [3] IV, 139 et seq.

for this movement was sent to three generals, one of whom " pinned it securely in an inside pocket," another memorized it " and then chewed it up," while the third lost it. The lost order was found and taken to McClellan, who after the signature of Lee's adjutant was verified, wrote to the President, " I have all the plans of the rebels and will catch them in their own trap if my men are equal to the emergency." [1] His men and officers were equal to the emergency but McClellan was not. The occasion demanded a celerity of movement of which he was incapable. He gained a partial victory in the Battle of Antietam but, at the time, it was sickening to think how much more might have been accomplished. The same reflection was inevitable in connexion with the battle itself. In the words of military critics it was, on the Union side, " a day of isolated attacks and wasted efforts "; the conduct of the battle " by Lee and his subordinates seems

---

[1] IV, 145 ; Hosmer, Appeal to Arms (Hart's American Nation), 189.

absolutely above criticism." [1]   Nevertheless
they retreated into Virginia. The two
armies then had an interval of rest before
renewing the active conflict which was des-
tined to be waged for another two and a
half-years.

In my account of the military movements
I have purposely fallen into the method of
the two combatants in obscuring the true
reason of the conflict. But this method
could not then nor can it now, be long persisted in, for both actor and historian find
themselves constantly running against the
reality behind the pretext. No one knew it
better than Lincoln but he gauged public
sentiment too well to be willing to change
the ostensible to the real purpose by public
avowal until the people were ready to follow
him. He turned a deaf ear to over-zealous
counsellors; he rescinded orders for the
emancipation of slaves issued by officious
generals; and all the while he was reflect-
ing how slavery might best be attacked.

[1] IV, 154.

Congress had prohibited slavery in all the existing territories and in any that should hereafter be acquired, thus enacting the principle which had led to the formation of the Republican party; in the District of Columbia, the seat of the national government, it had abolished slavery, with compensation for the owners of the slaves,[1] thereby taking a further step forward, which, on prudential grounds, had not been declared for in the two Republican national platforms. In March 1862, while fortune was prospering the Northern arms, the President suggested to Congress that they offer, on the part of the United States, pecuniary aid to any State that should adopt the gradual abolishment of slavery. Though it was hardly supposed that the Confederate States would heed the offer, it was nevertheless open to them all, and if anyone of them or all had, in this hour of Northern success, agreed to lay down their arms and respect the authority of the national government,

[1] III, 631.

no reasonable doubt can exist that they would have received, in a plan of gradual emancipation,[1] about four hundred dollars for each slave set free. The record of Lincoln and the Republican party on slavery is clear; their course was conservative and in line with the best traditions of England and America. Before Sumter was fired upon, they had practically agreed to guarantee in perpetuity the possession of slaves to their owners in all the slave States; now, after nearly a year of war and in the hour of victory, when the logic of events showed that slavery must go, they were willing to reimburse the slave owners, in spite of the detriment, both moral and material, which they had caused the common country.[2]

Mainly theoretical and entirely irrealizable as was this scheme, so far as it concerned the seceded States, it should have appealed to the border slave States that had

---

[1] "Gradual and not sudden emancipation is better for all." Lincoln's Message Mar. 6, 1862.

[2] III, 631, *et seq.*

remained in the Union as possessing a very
substantial practical value. Lincoln addressed them again and again urging them
with irrefutable argument and fervent appeal
to accept compensation for their slaves
while it was in his power to give it, but he
was unable to secure their assent to the
plan.[1] Bound up as was slavery with their
social and political life, they could not
understand that its doom was certain.
Then came the change in the military situation further stiffening their resistance.
Pending the discussion, the Northern successes of the spring were followed by Mc-
Clellan's disastrous failure in the Peninsula
and, during the ensuing interval of apprehension lest the cause of the North should
fail, the question arose of how much value
were the promises to pay of the United
States. The proposition was that the payment for the slaves should be made in six
per cent bonds, and, though Lincoln, it is
said, suggested that bonds were better prop-

[1] III, 631, 633; IV, 65, 67, 215.

erty than bondsmen,[1] many of the border
State men thought otherwise. But it is
certain that, if the border slave States had
acted promptly, they would have received
for their slaves a fair compensation in United
States bonds instead of having subsequently
to sustain a flat monetary loss through the
gift of freedom to the negroes.

Lincoln now began preparing for the ur-
gent and inevitable move whose " gravity,
importance and delicacy " demanded of him
the most earnest and careful study. During
the summer, a period of deep gloom at the
North, he had come to the conclusion that
since the slaves were growing the food for
the Confederate soldiers and serving as
teamsters and laborers on intrenchments in
the army service, " it was a military necessity, absolutely essential for the salvation
of the Union, that we must free the slaves
or be ourselves subdued." [2]   On July 22,
1862 he submitted to his Cabinet a proclamation embodying this idea but postponed

[1] IV, 218.   [2] IV, 69; Welles's Diary, I, 70.

its issue, because of an objection of Seward's, that, if it were now given to the country in the midst of our military disasters, it might be looked upon as " a cry for help, the government stretching forth its hands to Ethiopia " and as " our last *shriek* on the retreat." [1] Better wait, he argued, till it be supported by military success. Seeing the wisdom of Seward's objection, the President laid the draft of the proclamation aside.

The secret of this Cabinet meeting was strictly kept. The facts as known to-day furnish a curious commentary on Greeley's public complaint of twenty-nine days later which with characteristic egoism he entitled " The Prayer of Twenty Millions "; it was addressed to the President, and was based upon the assertion " that the Union cause is now suffering immensely from your mistaken deference to rebel slavery." This open letter gave Lincoln a chance through the press to iterate his policy which he

[1] IV, 72, *et ante.*

continued publicly to adhere to with con-
sistency. " My paramount object in this
struggle," he wrote, " is to save the Union
and is not either to save or to destroy slavery." On the other hand he wrote to a
Conservative, " I shall not surrender this
game leaving any available card unplayed."
From these and other utterances, during the
two months preceding a certain day sacred
in our annals, the working of Lincoln's mind
is open to us. At the Cabinet meeting of
September 22, 1862, after some general talk,
the President claimed the attention of his
ministers, reading from Artemus Ward's book
a chapter entitled " High-handed outrage at
Utica." He thought it very funny and enjoyed reading it, while the members of the
Cabinet, except the grave Secretary of War,
laughed with him. Lincoln then became
very serious and told of his reflections on
the slavery question since the July meeting.
Lee has been driven out of Maryland, he
said, and I am going to fulfil the promise
I made to myself and to my Maker. " I

have got you together to hear what I have written down. I do not wish your advice about the main matter; for that I have determined for myself." He read then his proclamation of freedom: "On the first day of January in the year of our Lord one thousand, eight hundred and sixty-three, all persons held as slaves within any State or designated part of a State, the people whereof shall then be in rebellion against the United States shall be then, henceforward, and forever free."[1]

[1] IV, 72, 157 *et ante*. Hay made this entry in his Diary on Sept. 23, 1862: "The President wrote the Proclamation on Sunday morning carefully. He called the Cabinet together on Monday, Sept. 22, made a little talk to them and read the momentous document." Later. "Chase [Secretary of the Treasury] spoke earnestly of the Proclamation. He said, 'This was a most wonderful history of an insanity of a class that the world had ever seen. If the slaveholders had staid in the Union, they might have kept the life in their institution for many years to come. That what no party and no public feeling in the North could ever have hoped to touch, they had madly placed in the very path of destruction.'" Letters and Diary of John Hay, I, 66, 67.

Welles under date of Sept. 22 wrote in his Diary concerning the Proclamation of Emancipation: "A favorable termination of this terrible conflict seems more remote with every movement, and unless the Rebels [as the Confederates were generally called at the North] hasten to avail themselves of the alternative presented, of which I see little probability, the war can scarcely be other than one of emancipation to the slave, or subjugation, or submission to their Rebel owners. There is in the Free States a very general impression that this measure will insure a speedy peace. I cannot say that I so view it. No one in those States dare advocate peace as a means of prolonging slavery, even if it is his honest opinion, and the pecuniary, industrial, and social sacrifice impending will intensify the struggle before us. While, however, these dark clouds are above and around us, I cannot see how the subject can be avoided. Perhaps it is not desirable it should be. It is, however, an arbitrary and despotic measure in the cause of freedom." I, 145.

It has always seemed to me a remarkable circumstance that Lincoln should have opened this Cabinet meeting by reading a chapter from Artemus Ward's book. There can be no question that he was very much impressed with the seriousness of the act he was about to perform. His summer had been full of perplexity and disappointment. Until Antietam he had had nothing but military failure. McClellan's Peninsular Campaign had come to naught. Lee's army had defeated the new general from the West, and, flushed with victory, had threatened Washington, Baltimore and Harrisburg. From a Confederate army in Kentucky, Cincinnati had been in imminent danger of capture and, at the time of this Cabinet meeting, Louisville stood in jeopardy. The President had hoped that McClellan would destroy Lee's army. The victory at Antietam simply turned back the Confederate invasion. That a man of deep feeling, who had had so much distress, who knew that the actors in great scenes of history ushered them in with gravity, generally with pomp and prayer, should have begun this solemn Cabinet meeting in a manner so grotesque, is extraordinary.

W. D. Howells writes in an Introduction to Artemus Ward's Best Stories (1912): " It must have been something more than the bad spelling which gave Artemus Ward's humor a currency beyond that of all other humorists before his time. . . . Men of my age will remember the universal joy in his fable of his interview with the Prince of Wales then visiting our States. . . . It must be owned that Artemus Ward had not Mark Twain's greatness of na-

K

ture, his generous scope, his actual humanity. . . .   He felt bound
to make you laugh first of all; Mark Twain felt bound to make
you laugh, too, but not always first of all; he might first wish to
make you feel. . . . In some of his beginnings Mark Twain
formed himself from, if not on, Artemus Ward. The imitation
could not last long; the great master was so immensely the
master. . . . We must remember how Lincoln loved Artemus
Ward and sought him in times of trouble when wiser and better
authorities could not have consoled him nearly so much. . . .
Artemus Ward's fame took him to England where probably the
happiest years of his short life were spent. Charles Reade called
him 'Artemus the delicious.' The English liked him with that
self abandon which wins the American heart, and made him so
wholly at home among them that, after some brief intervals in
America, he returned to die in England." Pp. viii, ix, xi, xiv, xv.

LECTURE III

THE first response of the country to Lincoln's Proclamation of Emancipation issued on September 22, 1862 was unfavorable. In the autumn elections, many of the important Northern States declared against the party in power, whose majority in the House of Representatives newly chosen was materially reduced.[1] The elections were characterized as a "vote of want of confidence" in the President, and to this result the Proclamation was undoubtedly a contributing force. But the dominant factor was the failure of our armies to accomplish decisive results in the field. Had McClellan captured or destroyed Lee's army at Antietam the President would have received at the ballot-box a triumphant

[1] IV, 163; Life of Morton, Foulke, I, 207.

approval of his whole policy. The defeat of the administration party in important States which was brought about by its former friends staying away from the polls, was a symptom of weariness of the war, a protest against the waste of so much life and money with an almost entire absence of results.

Lincoln made up his mind slowly. Nearly all his decisions were the outcome of careful deliberation, but, the decision once arrived at, he was thenceforth immovable. By gradual steps, he had come to the policy of emancipation and to it he was determined to stick in spite of the defeat of his party at the ballot-box and other discouraging events during the hundred days that intervened between the preliminary proclamation of September 22 and its necessary complement of January 1, 1863. Although the form of the preliminary proclamation implied that some of the Confederates or all might lay down their arms to avoid the loss of their slaves, no such outcome was seriously regarded as possible. Doubt no longer existed that a united people in the South were earnest in their desire to secure their independence and that, if the proclamation had affected them at all, it was to make them more determined than ever in their resistance by giving force to the argument that the war of the North was a crusade against their social institutions. Regarding the proclamation "as a fit and necessary war measure," the President wrote on January 1, 1863, "I do order and declare that all persons held as slaves" in the States or parts of States resisting the United States government "are, and henceforward shall be, free. . . .   Upon this act, sincerely believed to be an act of justice, warranted by the Constitution upon military necessity I invoke the considerate judgment of mankind and the gracious favor of Almighty God."[1]

[1] IV, 213 *et ante*.   "I am naturally anti-slavery," Lincoln wrote in a letter of Apr. 4, 1864.   "If slavery is not wrong nothing is wrong.   I cannot remember when I did not so think and feel, and

In spite of the expressed fears of unfriendly critics in England and in our own
country, the Proclamation did not excite

yet I have never understood that the presidency conferred upon
me an unrestricted right to act officially upon this judgment and
feeling. It was in the oath I took that I would, to the best of
my ability, preserve, protect and defend the Constitution of the
United States. I could not take the office without taking the oath.
Nor was it my view that I might take an oath to get power and
break the oath in using the power. I understood, too, that in
ordinary civil administration this oath even forbade me to practically indulge my primary abstract judgment on the moral question of slavery. I had publicly declared this many times and in
many ways. And I aver, that, to this day, I have done no official
act in mere deference to my abstract judgment and feeling on slavery.
I did understand, however, that my oath to preserve the Constitution to the best of my ability imposed upon me the duty of preserving, by every indispensable means, that government — that nation,
of which that Constitution was the organic law. . . . I felt that
measures otherwise unconstitutional might become lawful by
becoming indispensable to the preservation of the Constitution
through the preservation of the nation. Right or wrong, I assumed
this ground. . . . I could not feel that to the best of my ability,
I had even tried to preserve the Constitution, if, to save slavery or
any minor matter, I should permit the wreck of government,
country and Constitution all together. . . . When in March and
May and July, 1862, I made earnest and successive appeals to the
Border States to favor compensated emancipation, I believed the
indispensable necessity for military emancipation and arming
the blacks would come unless averted by that measure. They
declined the proposition and I was, in my best judgment, driven to
the alternative of either surrendering the Union, and with it the
Constitution, or of laying strong hand upon the colored element.
I chose the latter." Lincoln wrote in a letter of Aug. 26, 1863 : " I
think the Constitution invests its Commander-in-chief with the

servile insurrection,[1] although it completed
the process, which the war had begun, of
making every slave in the South a friend
of the North.   Every negro knew that if he
got within the lines of the Federal armies,

law of war in time of war.   The most that can be said — if so much
— is that slaves are property.   Is there — has there ever been— any
question that by the law of war, property, both of enemies and
friends, may be taken when needed ?   And is it not needed when-
ever taking it helps us, or hurts the enemy?   Armies, the world
over destroy enemies' property when they cannot use it ; and even
destroy their own to keep it from the enemy.   Civilized belligerents do all in their power to help themselves or hurt the enemy,
except a few things regarded as barbarous or cruel."   IV, 213, 214.

[1] The evidence warrants the oft-repeated statement that the
blacks made no move to rise.   " A thousand torches," Henry
Grady declared, "would have disbanded the Southern Army, but
there was not one."   Instead of rising they showed patient submission and fidelity to their owners.   It was their labor that produced food for the soldiers fighting to keep them in slavery and
without them the cotton could not have been raised which brought
supplies from Europe and the North.   Our great strength, declared
a Confederate official, consists in our system of slave labor because it "makes our 8,000,000 productive of fighting material equal
to the 20,000,000 of the North."   One owner or overseer to twenty
slaves was exempted from military service "to secure the proper
police of the country," but a study of the life indicates that he was
needed not for their restraint but for their intelligent direction.
As a matter of fact the able-bodied negroes were at home on the
plantation in the sparsely settled country of the Confederacy while
with few exceptions the white people in the neighborhood were old
or diseased men, women and children.   It is a wonderful picture,
one that discovers virtues in the Southern negroes and merit in the
civilization under which they had been trained.   V, 460, 461.

the aspiration of his life would be realized;
he would become a free man. Before the
close of the year 1863, there were in the
United States military service 100,000
former slaves, about one-half of which number actually bore arms in the ranks. But
for the policy of emancipation these negroes
would probably have remained at the South,
growing food for the able-bodied white men,
all of whom were forced into the Confederate army by the rigorous conscription.[1]

In addition to military emancipation, the
President proposed to give the slaves their
freedom in a strictly legal manner and to
insure the compensation of their owners by
the Federal government. In his annual
message to Congress of December 1, 1862,
he took as his text the sound and now
familiar proposition that " Without slavery
the rebellion [as he and the North called the
Civil War] could never have existed; without slavery it could not continue," and

[1] IV, 215. From 1863 to 1865, 180,000 negroes enlisted under
the Union flag. IV, 334.

showed in his argument a grasp of the subject which, in the light of our subsequent experience, has proved him a consummate statesman. He pleaded for gradual emancipation, appointing January 1, 1900, as the time when it should be completed to spare "both races from the evils of sudden derangement."[1] It is to be regretted that this prophetic appeal was not reënforced by victories in the field such as were wont to point the utterances of Cæsar and Napoleon.

[1] This plan, he argued, saves the slaves "from the vagrant destitution which must largely attend immediate emancipation in localities where their numbers are very great; and it gives the inspiring assurance that their posterity shall be free forever. It leaves to each State choosing to act under it to abolish slavery now, or at the end of the century, or at any intermediate time, or by degrees extending over the whole or any part of the period; and it obliges no two States to proceed alike. It also provides for compensation, and generally the mode of making it. . . . It is no less true for having been often said, that the people of the South are no more responsible for the original introduction of this property [property in slaves] than are the people of the North; and when it is remembered how unhesitatingly we all use cotton and sugar and share the profits of dealing in them, it may not be quite safe to say that the South has been more responsible than the North for its continuance. If, then, for a common object, this property is to be sacrificed, is it not just that it be done at a common charge?" Lincoln, Complete Works, II 272.

As matters stood, distrust of Lincoln pervaded both the Senate and the House and for the moment his personal prestige amongst the people had paled because his armies had made no headway; so it was hardly surprising that his policy of gradual and compensated emancipation failed to receive the approval of either Congress or the country. Nevertheless he had shown insight in seizing the moment of triumph to issue his Proclamation of Emancipation, as from Antietam in September 1862 to Gettysburg in July 1863 the North gained no real victory and her Army of the Potomac suffered two crushing defeats.

After Antietam the President again made strenuous effort to bring McClellan to the point of undertaking the vigorous offensive operations necessary for striking a decisive blow.[1]   At length his patience worn out by

[1] Welles under date of Oct. 18, 1862 wrote: "It is just five weeks since the Battle of Antietam and the army is quiet, reposing in camp. . . . The country groans. . . . McClellan is sadly afflicted with what the President calls the 'slows'."   Diary, I, 176.

the General's temperamental inability to reach an "ideal completeness of preparation," he removed him from the command of the Army of the Potomac.[1] His action would have been justifiable, had he known an officer equal or superior in military capacity to McClellan but although there were such men in the Army of the Potomac he had failed to discern them. He sent an order giving the command to Burnside, a man of winning personal qualities, who had twice refused it, deeming himself incompetent and McClellan the best fitted of all for the place. With deep regret Burnside obeyed the President's order and thenceforth did not enjoy a happy hour during the eighty days that he was in command. Promptly taking the offensive, he advanced his army across a river to make a frontal attack on Lee's soldiers, strongly intrenched

[1] IV, 188. Lee remarked to Longstreet that he regretted to part with McClellan, " for we always understood each other so well. I fear they may continue to make these changes until they find some one I don't understand." Hosmer, Appeal to Arms, 237.

and under his immediate direction.[1] The
Northern troops fought heroically and did
their best to carry out the foolhardy orders
but the only result was a terrible and useless slaughter of the flower of the army, the
Northern loss exceeding the Southern more
than twofold.

The day of this battle, wrote the correspondent of the *Times* from Lee's headquarters, will be " a memorable day to the
historian of the Decline and Fall of the
American Republic."[2] And so thought
many Northern people when they came to
know of the useless sacrifice of so many pre-
cious lives. During this period of gloom
and peril the writers of the day declared
that, an elastic and stout-hearted people
had been brought to the brink of despond-
ency; the North had lost heart and hope.
Greeley in the *New York Tribune* advocated
the mediation of a European power and the

---

[1] Battle of Fredericksburg, IV, 197 *et ante.*
[2] Issue of Jan. 13, 1863. The day of the battle was Dec.
13, 1862. IV, 200.

Emperor of the French offered his friendly offices for the purpose of bringing about an informal conference between the United and the Confederate States. The offer was at once declined but the certainty that Louis Napoleon was eager to interfere in the struggle deepened the gloom. The Democrats in a number of the Western States, weary of the war, threatened to inaugurate a movement in favor of an armistice which should lead to eventual peace. A prominent Western journalist, devoted to the Northern cause, feared that nothing was left but "to fight for a boundary."[1]

Lincoln was profoundly depressed. It was his general who had met this crushing defeat and he was responsible for it. So declared the Democrats without reserve. The Republicans, too in private conversation and confidential letters, showed that they held the same view, although in public they were cautious and reticent. Had ours been a government of the responsible-ministry

[1] IV, 222, 223.

type, Congress, which was then in session, would have voted a want of confidence in Lincoln ; and this was the one period during his term of office, when it was just doubtful if the country would have sustained him. But our President is elected for a fixed period of four years and Lincoln had not yet served half his term. In his own words uttered in an earlier and less grave crisis, "There is no way in which I can have any other man put where I am. I am here. I must do the best I can and bear the responsibility of taking the course which I feel I ought to take."[1]   Congress recognized its limitations ; it could not remove Lincoln from office and it agreed with him that the war must be prosecuted to the end. It gave him therefore the sword and purse of the nation, passing a rigorous conscription law and a drastic financial act, astounding in its magnitude of provision for the enormous expenses of the war.[2]

Burnside, full of human sympathy, was

[1] IV, 203.   [2] IV, 236.

wild with grief at his disaster. "Oh those
men! Those men over there!" he said,
pointing across the river where lay the dead
and wounded, "I am thinking of them all
the time." In a turn of frenzied energy, he
made plans for an advance impossible of
execution. A new general was imperatively
needed. The President relieved Burnside
and placed Hooker in command of the Army
of the Potomac.

A preëminent leader and representative
of popular sentiment, such as Lincoln, in-
curs a risk in handling military affairs inasmuch as in time of stress he may set too
high a value on the voice of the people
which is not often successful in designating
a commander of genius and skill. In the
appointment of Hooker he put in force the
opinion of the country and of the rank and
file of the army, which had been formed in
accordance with the general's record as an
excellent and dashing corps commander.
"Fighting Joe" was the name that he had
won and in the anxious search for a leader,

it was not unnatural that he was selected. Nevertheless, though Lincoln was a better judge of military affairs than any of his advisers taken from civil life and though he is entitled in this painful crisis to the historian's most charitable treatment, it is evident, from the facts known at the time, that the choice of Hooker was unwarrantable. For in the general of a democratic army nothing but transcendent ability can make up for lack of personal character; and Hooker was deficient in both respects.

Nevertheless he was a good organizer, put heart into the dispirited army and stopped desertions which of late had been alarmingly frequent. Towards the end of April 1863, satisfied that his army was fit for action he set forth on his Chancellorsville campaign with 130,000 men to Lee's 60,000 and, after a capital beginning, lost nerve and was completely outgeneralled by Lee. Lee knew Hooker better than Lincoln did and showed his contempt of the enemy by dividing his army, and sending

Jackson, "the great flanker," on a forced march to attack Hooker's right which was surprised and put to confusion. In the ensuing three days' battle, Lee utterly defeated Hooker[1] but sustained an irreparable loss in the death of Stonewall Jackson, who, by a mischance that the South never ceased to lament, was shot by his own men.

After his army had been given a rest of some weeks Lee, believing that nothing was to be gained by "remaining quietly on the defensive,"[2] began an invasion of the North, undoubtedly hoping to defeat the Union army, capture Washington and dictate a peace or secure European recognition of the Southern Confederacy. He soon had an army of 75,000 on Pennsylvania soil causing intense alarm throughout the North. Every Northern man took up his morning news-

[1] IV, 264 *et ante*. Welles made this entry under date of May 6, 1863: "Sumner came into my room, and raising both hands exclaimed, 'Lost, lost, all is lost!' I asked what he meant. He said Hooker and his army had been defeated and driven back to this side of the Rappahannock. Sumner came direct from the President, who, he said, was extremely dejected." Diary, I, 293.

[2] IV, 268.

paper with misgiving, and watched with
growing alarm the periodical bulletins that
told of the progress northward of the Confederate army.[1] At this juncture, the Northern cause received a blessing in the disguise of
a dispute between Hooker and the President's
chief of staff. Hooker asked to be relieved
from command and the President, taking him
at his word, at once put Meade, a true soldier,
in his place. Lee rated Meade higher than
Hooker, but thought that the change of
commanders at this critical moment over-
balanced the advantage in generalship.
He had undoubtedly become persuaded that
he and his army were invincible, and this

[1] Welles under date of June 15, 1863 wrote: "Something of a
panic pervades the city [Washington]. Singular rumors reach us
of Rebel advances into Maryland. . . . There is trouble, confusion,
uncertainty, where there should be calm intelligence. I have a
panic telegraph from Governor Curtin, [Pennsylvania], who is ex-
citable and easily alarmed, entreating that guns and gunners may
be sent from the navy yard at Philadelphia to Harrisburg without
delay. . . . Hooker does not comprehend Lee's intentions nor
know how to counteract them. . . . It looks to me as if Lee was
putting forth his whole energy and force in one great and desper-
ate struggle which shall be decisive; that he means to strike a
blow that will be severely felt, and of serious consequences, and
thus bring the War to a close." Diary, I, 329, 330.

confidence was shared by nearly all of his officers and men. The two armies met at Gettysburg, Pennsylvania, and fought for three days. On the first two days, the advantage was with Lee. Meade was loyally supported by his corps commanders and in a council of war at the end of the second day, although having to reckon with a loss of 20,000 men, or more than one-fifth of his army, all voted to "stay and fight it out."[1]

On the third day, after a terrific and prolonged cannonade, Lee ordered the famous Pickett charge. Under the hot sun of a July afternoon, 15,000 men issued from the Confederate position to cross the open valley, nearly a mile wide, that separated them from the enemy. They received first a devastating fire from Meade's batteries, then a storm of canister and, as they drew nearer, the steady fusillade of the infantry. The slaughter was terrible, only

[1] For a clear statement of the disadvantages under which Meade labored, see C. F. Adams, Studies Military and Diplomatic, 309. For an account of the Gettysburg campaign, IV, 268 *et seq*.

a few men reached the Union lines. The
Confederates were forced to retreat. On
account of the failure of this charge, Lee's
second and last invasion of the North had
come to naught. His loss at Gettysburg
was 28,000 to Meade's 23,000.[1]

At the same hour on July 4 (1863), when
the President announced the result of the
battle of Gettysburg to the country, Vicksburg, a strong fortress on the Mississippi
river and, after Richmond, the most important one in the Confederacy, surrendered to
General Grant. This event was the cul-
mination of the most brilliant offensive
campaign of the war. Many and various
attempts had been made to capture this
redoubtable stronghold and finally Grant
conceived a plan which no other Northern
general would have had the hardihood to
execute. " I became satisfied," he said,
" that Vicksburg could only be turned from
the south side." [2]   Crossing the Mississippi

---

[1] Livermore, Numbers and Losses, 102.   The battle of Gettysburg took place July 1, 2, 3, 1863.   [2] Nicolay, Hay, VII, 146.

above Vicksburg which is on the east bank,
he marched to a point south of it on the
west bank where he was dependent on the
navy for indispensable supplies. He had
reckoned on efficient support on the river
and was not to be disappointed; gunboats
with transports heavily loaded with supplies
succeeded in running past the Confederate
batteries of Vicksburg. His next projected
movement must be conducted for the most
part, in a swamp formed by the river with
its many bayous and now become unusually
difficult of passage because of heavy spring
rains and neglected and broken levees.
High ground on the east bank must be
reached somehow; and when Grant with
unflagging energy had succeeded in putting
this formidable problem behind him, a feeling of relief and confident expectancy
possessed him such as he rarely experienced
in his subsequent military career. "The
battle is now more than half won," he telegraphed to Washington. Nevertheless he
had still to advance in the face of certain

opposition through a country where swamps, cane-brakes and forests choked with undergrowth and trailing shrubs followed one upon another in disheartening continuity. Nothing daunted he cut loose from his base and set out to meet the enemy who, in the theatre of operations outnumbered him. Moving with extraordinary rapidity and throwing upon each detachment of the Confederates a superior force, he defeated them in detail and cleared the way to his final objective point.   Within nineteen days [1] from his recrossing of the Mississippi to the east bank in the enemy's territory Grant had marched a hundred and eighty miles through a most difficult country — skirmishing constantly, winning five separate battles, inflicting greater loss than he sustained, destroying arsenals and capturing cannon — and, on May 18, had taken possession of the dry high ground north of Vicksburg, securing a base of supplies which had safe and unobstructed water communication

[1] April 30–May 18, 1863.

with the North.[1]   He then invested the city
with engineering skill.

Throughout the campaign the President
had given Grant faithful support and he
now sent him reënforcements adequate to
defeat any attempt at a relief of the garrison.   Jefferson Davis made strenuous
efforts to save his important fortress but,
after draining the resources of the Confederacy, he could not furnish his general with
a sufficient force to justify an attack upon
Grant.   The garrison of Vicksburg was
starved into capitulation.[2]

Gettysburg and Vicksburg were great
victories.   Had the war been one between
two nations, it would now have undoubtedly
terminated in a treaty of peace, with conditions imposed largely by the more successful combatant.

Trade relations with Europe were of such
a character that the North and the South
could not fight their battle out without refer-

[1] IV, 309 *et ante.*   [2] IV, 310 *et seq.*

ence to conditions abroad, and, for moral as well as material reasons, England was the predominant influence. She had opposed slavery and the North looked to her for sympathy. On the other hand the Southerners desired material aid and believed that their great staple would compel it. Cotton is King, they declared. England must have it to keep her factories going and give her operatives bread; she will be eager to exchange for cotton her manufactured goods which we greatly need.[1] The South was disappointed. England issued the usual proclamation of neutrality but went no further. Nor was the North, at first, any better pleased with the proclamation, since no nation likes to see those whom it calls rebels accorded belligerent rights. But as Davis had invited applications for letters of marque and Lincoln had proclaimed a blockade of the Southern ports, it seemed to the Eng-

[1] "With their cotton, the Confederates were like Archimedes with his lever, confident that they could move the world if they once got a place to stand on." Frederic Bancroft, Life of Seward, II, 289.

lish government that a state of war existed which must be formally recognized.[1] Whilst considerable dissatisfaction was expressed in the North at the so-called "precipitate" concession of belligerency to the Confederate States and condemnation of it bulks large in the later discussion, England was not actuated by unfriendly feeling to the North and, according to international practice, may be abundantly justified for her action.[2] And as soon as the wide difference between the concession of belligerent rights and a recognition of the independence of the Confederacy was appreciated, both President and people saw that there was, as yet, no ground of complaint against Great Britain. At the same time, the English had a true conception of the conflict. Lord John Russell's declaration in the House of Commons that the trouble had " arisen from that accursed

[1] III, 417. All the important powers of Europe followed substantially the action of Great Britain.

[2] III, 420; VI, 365 n. 1; C. F. Adams, The Treaty of Washington, in Lee at Appomattox, 96; also paper read before Massachusetts Historical Society, November, 1911; Bancroft, Life of Seward, II, 176.

institution of slavery" was generally approved; and Charles Francis Adams, our minister to England noted on May 31, 1861 that the favorable feeling toward the United States among the people at large had extended to the higher circles.[1] "I have not seen or heard of a soul," wrote Charles Darwin in a private letter on June 5 [1861] "who is not with the North."[2]   But Palmerston perceived a divided duty saying with cynical frankness to an American, "We do not like slavery but we want cotton and we dislike very much your Morrill tariff."[3] This tariff, enacted after the secession of the Southern senators, was regarded in England as a measure of high protection to American manufacturers.

If the initial victory had been gained by the North, the friendly feeling would doubtless have persisted and grown, but the South won the first battle and, when the story of Bull Run became known, a marked revulsion

[1] III, 426, 429.   [2] III, 502.
[3] July 30.   III, 433.

of sentiment took place. The prominent public men distinctly favorable to the South were balanced by the outspoken friends of the North amongst whom were Bright, Cobden, William E. Forster, the Duke of Argyll and Thomas E. Hughes; but the main body of the aristocracy and middle class thought that the Union could not conquer the Confederacy and earnestly longed for the war to cease. The aristocracy willingly believed that the " bubble of democracy had burst in America," aware as they were that a divided Union would be less of a moral menace than a compact democratic federal government to the intrenched rights, on which the polity of Great Britain was based. In the middle class merchants and manufacturers were in dire straits because the supply of cotton was cut off. General business was deranged in consequence. Thousands of workingmen saw hunger staring them in the face whilst the well-to-do were alarmed at the prospect of curtailed incomes demanding a sacrifice of luxuries and even some of the adjuncts of comfortable existence. Goldwin Smith, a friend to the North, was justified in describing the state of affairs as " The awful peril not only commercial but social with which the cotton famine threatened us and the thrill of alarm and horror which upon the dawning of that peril ran through the whole land." [1]   Peace would open the Southern ports, cotton would again come to England; and as the great body of voting Liberals and Conservatives believed that the South was certain in the end to gain her independence, the sooner that fact was acknowledged by the North, the better. This doctrine found able exponents in Palmerston and Russell, the two leading men of the Cabinet and received the powerful support of the *Times* and the *Saturday Review*. " The people of the Southern States," declared the *Times*, " may be wrong but they are ten millions." [2]   Although the

[1] III, 503. " Excepting the Irish famine, the country had seen no such distress for a century." Bancroft, Life of Seward, II, 302.

[2] III, 509 *et ante*. In fact only nine millions, five and one-half million whites, three and one half million negroes.

Times here slightly exaggerated their numbers it was right in implying that they were a formidable people to subdue. On the other hand the South attracted sympathy because she was the weaker party and was making a fight for independence as the Italians had done in their War of Liberation of 1859.

Short-sightedness and the sting of defeat were responsible for our government and people committing a blunder which tended further to alienate the country whose sympathy was so much desired. England was under the reign of the ten-pounders when the *Times* had an almost overpowering influence on the governing opinion.[1] Though Delane had become a partisan of the South, his correspondent in America, William H. Russell, differed from him and presented in his correspondence a view opposed to that of the editor and his leader-writers. Before actual fighting began, he made a journey through the Southern States, writing graphic and impartial letters, in which he told the

[1] IV, 83.

English public in unmistakable terms that the cause of the South was the cause of the slave power. Detesting slavery as he did, he gave an account of a slave auction witnessed by himself under the shadow of the Capitol, in which the Confederate Congress was sitting, which was worth reams of journalistic argument. A stout young man of five and twenty was being knocked down for nine hundred and seventy-five dollars. "I am neither sentimentalist," Russell wrote, " nor Black Republican, nor negro-worshipper, but I confess the sight caused a strange thrill through my heart. I tried in vain to make myself familiar with the fact that I could for the sum of nine hundred and seventy-five dollars, become as absolutely the owner of that mass of blood, bones, sinew, flesh and brains as of the horse which stood by my side. There was no sophistry which could persuade me the man was not a man; he was indeed by no means my brother, but assuredly he was a fellow creature."[1] With

[1] Letter to the *Times* from Montgomery, May 8, 1861. III, 431 n.

due appreciation, Adams spoke of Russell's letters as swaying opinion in favor of the North.[1]   And it was not Delane who called this sound and able writer home.   We drove him away.

Russell saw the Union forces retreating in panic after the battle of Bull Run and wrote an interesting and accurate report of his experience.   If his letter had appeared immediately in the Northern newspapers it would have been regarded merely as the best written account of the affair but a month elapsed before the *Times*, in which it was printed, reached America.   Then over-sensitive ones who had been chewing the cud of defeat read into it a sneer at the supposed cowardice of the Northern troops and imposed this interpretation on the public generally, who henceforth spoke disparagingly of " Bull Run Russell."   Our friend's position was made uncomfortable, and his enemies were on the alert to seize hold of anything that might compromise

[1] June 21.   III, 431.

him.   Unearthing a telegram, they accused
him of having betrayed confidential informa-
tion from the British Embassy for the purpose of speculating in Wall street.   His
explanation was entirely satisfactory and, in
in any case, the aggrieved parties were the
British Embassy and the *Times*.   Convinced
that Russell had been, at the worst, merely
indiscreet, Delane wished him to remain in
America, but owing to the unfriendly feeling which had grown up around him and
the base use that was made of this unfortunate incident, he was hampered in getting
permits to accompany the army.   Conclud-
ing that his usefulness was at an end he
went home.[1]

The ostracism of Russell meant a loss to
our cause in so far as it depended upon a
correct English appreciation.   He early
recognized Lincoln's parts and would have
rejoiced in the delineation of his growing

[1] Russell in a private letter to Delane wrote on Oct. 14, 1861,
" The Americans, with all their faults, are a prodigious fine peo-
ple, and I cannot help admiring many things about them." —
Atkins, Life of W. H. Russell, II, 85.

power as he grappled with slavery[1] and moved generals and armies to final triumph. Grateful as was the North for the support of the *Daily News* and *Spectator*, Russell's letters in the *Times* would have been an additional and powerful influence. The President ought indubitably to have interfered in Russell's behalf. In their first interview he spoke of the *Times* as one of the greatest powers in the world. But after the Bull Run letter he "looked as black as thunder" so Russell wrote, and later explained his coldness by the remark, "You represent the *Times* which has shown such a bitter enmity to the United States."[2] Before the end of 1861 we committed a stiil greater blunder in not disavowing promptly the act of an "ambitious, self-conceited and self-willed"[3] naval captain. Wilkes, in command of an American man-

[1] Russell wrote privately Dec. 20, 1861, "I am much exercised about the Southern people becoming independent and a slave power." — Atkins, Life of W. H. Russell, II, 89.

[2] Atkins, Life of W. H. Russell, II, 76, 85.

[3] Welles's Diary, I, 87.

of-war stopped the British mail steamship *Trent* in the Bahama channel and took from her by force Mason and Slidell, commissioners from the Southern Confederacy to Great Britain and France, then on their way from Havana to Southampton. He heeded neither their appeal to the British flag for protection nor the protest of a Captain of the royal navy in charge of the mails. When the news of this incident was received in New York (Nov. 16, 1861) the country went as wild with jubilant delight as if a great victory had been won in the field. I remember going, when a boy of thirteen, to a war meeting in Cleveland and hearing the thunders of applause which greeted a mention of this capture as an important success. The Northern people had waited and watched so long for some result from the immense levies of men and of money that no rejoicing could seem excessive when they saw two of their hated enemies — the one author of the Fugitive Slave Law, the other champion of filibustering in the interest of slavery — delivered into their hands. The Secretary of the Navy sent Wilkes a congratulatory letter. Boston gave him a banquet, at which the Governor of Massachusetts and the Chief Justice of her Supreme Court praised his action. The national House of Representatives, on the first day of its session thanked him "for his brave, adroit and patriotic conduct." His act was justified by lawyers and statesmen. Two public men however pointed out the only correct course open to the government. Of the captives, Senator Sumner said at once "We shall have to give them up." [1] Montgomery Blair, a member of the cabinet recommended that Wilkes be ordered to take Mason and Slidell on a war-ship to England and deliver them to the English government.[2] The President at first perceived clearly the national obligation. "I fear these men will prove to be white elephants," he said. "We must stick to American principles

[1] Pierce's Sumner, IV, 52.   [2] III, 523.

concerning the rights of neutrals."[1] He
ought to have had more confidence in his
power of leading public sentiment and trans-
formed his words into action. For it would
have been grateful and astute, honorable
and politic to have delivered up Mason and
Slidell before the English government made
a peremptory demand for them. Such action would have lent an irresistible force
to all our subsequent entreaties to England
to observe scrupulously her neutrality or
rather it would have rendered such entreaties needless, since the fact of standing by
our own precedents, when they went against
us, would have won the respect due to a
far-sighted international deed and insured
us the friendly neutrality of Great Britain.
Instead of being at once surrendered, Mason
and Slidell were confined as prisoners in
Fort Warren, Boston harbor. But for the
extreme tension existing generally in Northern minds as a result of weary expectation
and repeated disappointment, the President

[1] Lossing's Civil War, II, 156.

and his advisers would undoubtedly have
realized, as did the *Times* that, " the voices
of these Southern commissioners, sounding
from their captivity, are a thousand times
more eloquent in London and Paris than
they would have been if heard at St. James's
and the Tuileries." [1]

The news made a great sensation in England; the opinion was general that the
arrest of Mason and Slidell was an outrage
on the flag. According to English precedents and abstract legal reasoning from
them, the act of Wilkes might be justified,[2]
but face to face with the concrete fact in
1861, anybody could see that no strong
neutral power with a large merchant marine
could permit a belligerent to stop and search
its ships and seize emissaries of the enemy
who had trusted to the protection of the
flag. The English Cabinet decided that the
act of Captain Wilkes was " a clear violation

[1] Nov. 28, III, 523.

[2] C. F. Adams, Military and Diplomatic Studies, 398; Paper
read before the Mass. Hist. Soc. Nov. 1911; Dasent's Delane, II, 36.

of the law of nations and one for which reparation must be at once demanded." Earl Russell prepared a despatch to Lord Lyons, the British minister in Washington, the language of which was softened and made more friendly at the suggestion of the Queen and Prince Consort, but even as modified, the British government's demand was for the liberation of Mason and Slidell and "a suitable apology for the aggression."[1] As there was as that time no cable between England and America, the despatch was sent to Washington by a Queen's messenger and reached the Secretary of State through the usual diplomatic channel. The President and his Cabinet carefully considered the demand, saw the justice of it and delivered Mason and Slidell to an English steamer. The disavowal of the act was accepted as a sufficient apology.[2]

Considering the intense feeling on both sides of the Atlantic, each government acted moderately and with dignity. In the flush

[1] III, 525.   [2] III, 538 *et ante*.

of excitement, American jingoes were conspicuous, talking recklessly of their desire to fight the traditional enemy, seeming to ignore in their boasts the certainty that war with Great Britain would mean that we must abandon our effort to defeat the South. In England during the first explosion, the active sympathizers with the South were eager to embroil the two countries but a large majority wished a peaceful settlement [1] and did not contemplate with satisfaction an alliance with a slave power. Such was undoubtedly the opinion of nearly all those persons to whom the *Times* was either an organ or an oracle, although the editor himself held the opposite view. There is a "real, downright, honest desire to avenge

[1] Robert Browning wrote to W. W. Story on Dec. 31, 1861: "I have not heard one man, woman or child express anything but dismay at the prospect of being obliged to go to war on any grounds with America; but every one felt there might be an obligation as stringent as a slap on the face in public from one's bosom friend." Henry James, Life of Story, II, 109.

On our side, Charles Eliot Norton wrote on the same day to George W. Curtis: "Shall we yet have to fight England? With all my heart I hope not, — but if need be I am ready." *Atlantic Monthly*, Nov. 1912, 605.

old scores," wrote Delane in a private letter.
" The whole Army, Navy and Volunteers are
of one mind and all mad for service in
America." [1] The seizure, our neglect to
surrender Mason and Slidell at once, our
popular approval of Wilkes lost us likewise
the good will of friends. " I agree with
you," wrote Darwin to Sir Joseph Hooker
on January 25, 1862, " the present American row has a very Toryfying influence on
us all." [2] On the other hand the intensity
on our side is seen in its survival in James
Russell Lowell, who wrote seven years later :
" It is the *Trent* that we quarrel about, like
Percy and Glendower. That was like an
east wind to our old wound and set it
atwinge once more. . . . That imperious
despatch of Lord John's made all those inherited drops of ill-blood as hot as present
wrongs." [3]

[1] Atkins, Life of W. H. Russell, II, 88.
[2] III, 543.
[3] III, 542, see especially note 2. Excellent accounts of the
Trent affair are in C. F. Adams's Life of Charles Francis Adams
and in his paper read before the Mass. Historical Society at the

In international differences, the blunders are rarely confined to one side. The neglect of the British government to detain the war steamers *Florida* and *Alabama*, which were built in 1862 for the Southern Confederacy, were violations of the neutrality which had been formally declared. The case of the *Alabama* was the more flagrant of the two. The story of her building and escape is a long one which may not be related here. I will, however, mention the declarations of three eminent Englishmen. Sir Robert Collier, Queen's Counsel, whose opinion had been asked by Adams, our minister, said, before the *Alabama* got away, It is the duty of the collector of customs in Liverpool to detain the *Alabama*. "It appears difficult to make out a stronger case of infringement of the Foreign Enlistment Act, which if not enforced on this occasion is little better than a dead letter." Chief

November meeting of 1911; and in Chapter XXXIII of Bancroft's Life of Seward. See also R. H. Dana's paper read before the Mass. Historical Society at the March meeting of 1912.

Justice Cockburn the English member of the Geneva Tribunal, declared,[1] It was the duty of the Commissioners of Customs, to whom as his superiors the Collector had referred the matter, "to direct the seizure" of the *Alabama*. Earl Russell, the highest in authority, wrote in after years with a candor which does him honor, "I ought to have been satisfied with the opinion of Sir Robert Collier and to have given orders to detain the *Alabama* at Birkenhead."[2]

The military reverses during the summer of 1862 confirmed the majority of English voters in their opinion that the North could not conquer the South, and this opinion was shared by many of our friends. "There is an all but unanimous belief that you *cannot* subject the South to the Union," wrote Cobden to Sumner. "I feel quite convinced that unless cotton comes in considerable quantities before the end of the year, the governments of Europe will be

[1] In 1872.   [2] IV, 88 *et ante.*

knocking at your door." [1] The cotton famine was then at its height [2] and Cobden's fears came near realization. Since the autumn of 1861, Louis Napoleon had been eager for the coöperation of England in recognizing the independence of the Southern Confederacy and breaking the blockade or, if she would not go so far, in an offer of mediation; he wanted cotton and moreover desired the backing of the South in his Mexican adventure. Palmerston, in touch with his majority in the House and with the voters who elected it, wrote to Earl Russell on September 14, 1862, "The Federals got a very complete smashing" and if Washington or Baltimore "fall into the hands of the Confederates" as "seems not altogether unlikely" should not England and France "address the contending parties and recommend an agreement upon the basis of separation?"

[1] July 11, 1862, IV, 85 n.

[2] To be exact it was at its height during the summer and autumn of 1862, IV, 84 n., 363 n.; Bancroft, Life of Seward, II, 302.

Russell agreed and suggested a meeting of
the cabinet to consider the matter. Palmerston, however, as he watched the sequence
of events, realized that the Northern victory
of Antietam had a considerable effect on
the British public; he therefore counselled
a brief delay.[1] Now Gladstone, the third
member in importance in the Cabinet, came
to the front. Having been informed by
Palmerston of his and Russell's view of the
course which ought to be taken by the
English government and having expressed
his concurrence in it with the added suggestion that the proceedings be prompt, Gladstone took the public into the government's
confidence in his celebrated speech in Newcastle on October 7, and, in the light of his
own carefully matured opinion, emphasized
what he thought was the definite conclusion
of the ministry. "There is no doubt," he
declared, "that Jefferson Davis and other
leaders of the South have made an army;
they are making, it appears, a navy; and

[1] IV, 338, 339.

they have made what is more than either
— they have made a nation. We may
anticipate with certainty the success of the
Southern States so far as their separation
from the North is concerned." [1] The construction which the country naturally put
upon this speech was that the government
had determined on the recognition of the
Southern Confederacy. If I had entirely
trusted to this construction, said Adams
later to Earl Russell, " I should have begun
to think of packing my carpet-bag and
trunks." [2] And for the moment Gladstone
seemed indeed to have proclaimed the
government's policy. Six days later (October 13), Russell sent to his colleagues a confidential memorandum, inquiring " whether
it is not a duty for Europe to ask both
parties in the most friendly and conciliatory
terms to agree to a suspension of arms,"
and appointing October 23 for a Cabinet
meeting to consider the question. But the
next day after the despatch of Russell's

[1] IV, 339.   [2] IV, 339, 341.

communication, Sir George Cornewall Lewis, the member of the Cabinet ranking next in importance to Gladstone, made a speech at Palmerston's request, which plainly left the inference to be drawn that the government had no intention of recognizing the independence of the Southern States.[1] It is not clear why Palmerston so suddenly changed his mind nor why he did not notify Earl Russell, so as to prevent the issuing of the confidential memorandum. At all events, the appointed Cabinet meeting was not held and it was informally determined that the existing policy of non-intervention should be continued.[2] A month later the English government declined to join the Emperor of the French in an offer of mediation between the South and the North.[3]

[1] IV, 341; Morley's Gladstone, II, 80; Adams's Military and Diplomatic Studies, 409.

[2] IV, 343; Dip. Corr., 223, 225–226; Adams's Military and Diplomatic Studies, 410; Mass. His. Soc. 2d ser. XX, 469; The Times, Oct. 24, 1862 citing Globe of Oct. 23.

[3] IV, 347.

It was certainly not Lincoln's preliminary proclamation of emancipation which prevented a change of policy on the part of the Palmerston-Russell ministry for the governing classes generally regarded this pronouncement as calculated to excite servile insurrection.[1] Far otherwise from the ten-pounders, who may have numbered a million, opined the five million men who did not possess the franchise.[2] These, almost to a man, applauded the proclamation and admired its author. When it came to be fully understood and when the supplementary edict of January 1, 1863 had established it as a fixed policy, large public meetings were held all over England in support of emancipation and every mention of Lincoln's name was greeted with cheers. "God bless and strengthen the North; give victory to their arms!" prayed Spurgeon to his congregation of many thousands. A large delegation of anti-slavery people left

[1] IV, 343; Adams, Life of C. F. Adams, 291.
[2] John Bright, Speeches, II, 191; IV, 358.

me, so Adams wrote, "with hearty shakes
of the hand that marked the existence of
active feeling at bottom, the genuine English heartiness of good will." [1]

How the common people of England differed from the people of means and education in their estimate of Lincoln was a
striking feature of the situation. An English friend of William H. Russell's, who had
accompanied him in a visit to the army
headquarters in Washington, asked, "Why
did you stand up when that tall fellow in
the shooting suit came into the room?"
"Because it was the President." "The
President of what?" "Of the United
States!" Oh! come now, you're hum-
bugging me. Let me have another look
at him." Another look was followed by
the exclamation, "I give up the United
States!" [2] The Marquis of Hartington saw
Lincoln a few days after the issue of the
Proclamation of Emancipation and wrote
thus to his father: "I never saw such a

---

[1] IV, 351, 354.   [2] Atkins, Life of W. H. Russell, II, 83.

specimen of a Yankee in my life. I should think he was a very well meaning sort of a man but, almost every one says, about as fit for his position now as a fire shovel." [1] In a letter of February 1863, Hartington shows the contrast between the sentiment of his class and that of the common people. "I am decidedly very Southern in the main," he wrote, "and from what I see, that would not at all suit my constituents. How they can be so idiotic as to admire Lincoln and his Emancipation Proclamation and how they can talk such nonsense as they do about emancipation I cannot understand and I shall have to tell them so." [2]

In our own country as well Lincoln's hold was on the plain people. Not in Washington did one find his unvarying admirers. His undignified bearing, grotesqueness of speech and manner — still more his proneness to jocularity when others were depressed — proved severely trying to seri-

[1] Sept. 29, 1862. Holland, Life of the Duke of Devonshire, I, 43.
[2] Ibid, I, 53.

N

ous men who were anxious for the safety of the State. There were senators and representatives and at least one member of his cabinet who had a profound contempt for his supposed ability and were undisguisedly repelled by his daily walk and conversation; but the soldiers and sailors, the operatives of New England, the iron workers in Pittsburg and the farmers of the West, who knew him by his State papers, letters and speeches developed for him a respect and affectionate sympathy which never lessened but almost constantly grew.[1]

If the North could have had military success early in 1863, the uprising of the English common people in her favor would have settled the policy of the English government, but in the actual sequence of events, the dep-

[1] IV, 210. "Homely, honest, ungainly Lincoln," wrote Asa Gray to Darwin on Feb. 16, 1864, "is the representative man of the country." IV, 461. There was a similar development of opinion in England. On Nov. 20, 1863, John Bright wrote to Sumner: "It is remarkable that in this country all parties have a high respect for Lincoln — so much does a real integrity gain upon the minds of all men." Mass. Hist. Soc. Proceedings XLVI, 127.

redations of the Alabama, almost sweeping our flag from the seas, together with the construction of three more war-ships at Liverpool and Birkenhead, intended for Confederate cruisers, brought the two countries to the brink of war. In a correspondence with Earl Russell that was not wholly free from acerbity, Adams persistently urged upon the English government its responsibility for the destruction caused by the Alabama. Whilst Russell on behalf of his government disclaimed all responsibility, he nevertheless believed that he had been tricked in the affair of the vessel's escape; and his action in 1863 was the action of a friendly neutral. He stopped the gunboat Alexandra which was intended for the Southern Confederacy. Then peace or war depended upon the seizure of two ironclad rams building at Birkenhead, which, if suffered to escape as did the Alabama, might break the blockade, ascend the Potomac, render Washington uninhabitable and lay Philadelphia under contribution. The Confederate agent was astute and made an adroit effort to conceal the real ownership.[1]   The deceitful transfer of the vessels and the judicial construction of the statute in the case of the Alexandra [2] hedged Earl Russell about with difficulties, but quickened by an honest purpose, he perceived, through the meshes of intrigue, that the ironclad rams were intended for the Southern Confederacy and directed that they be detained.   Eventually they were purchased by the British Admiralty.[3]

We were fortunate in our minister to England, Charles Francis Adams, whose diplomatic course was almost faultless.   He won the respect and liking of Lord Russell and came to be highly esteemed in London society.   After Russell in the affair of the

---

[1] He had sold the rams to a French firm who had engaged themselves to resell them to him when they should get beyond British jurisdiction.

[2] The Lord Chief Baron of the Court of Exchequer decided that the government had no right to seize the gunboat.

[3] IV, 384 *et ante*.   Adams, Life of Charles F. Adams, 315 ; Bancroft, Life of Seward, II, 303, 314, p. 383 *et seq.*   Stopping these ironclads " is a question of life or death."   Assistant Secretary of the Navy Fox, Life of J. M. Forbes, II, 23.

Alexandra had determined on a friendly neutrality, the victories of Gettysburg and Vicksburg came to strengthen his hand in the seizure of the ironclad rams. Thenceforward there was no danger of foreign intervention in our conflict.

If, in reviewing the attitude of foreign powers, the policy of the Emperor of the French be contrasted with that of the government of Great Britain the latter appears to border on friendliness. England indeed was the insurmountable obstacle to the recognition of the Southern Confederacy by France and other European nations.[1]

---

[1] IV, 388. In September 1864, Benjamin the Secretary of State of the Southern Confederacy, wrote: " The English government has scarcely disguised its hostility. From the commencement of the struggle it has professed a newly invented neutrality which it had frankly defined as meaning a course of conduct more favorable to the stronger belligerents." Bancroft presenting a careful Northern view makes this comment: " The offence of the British government was that it did not use due diligence to prevent the departure of the Confederate ships or to detain them when they came within colonial ports. The attitude of the French government was very different. . . . Napoleon suggested to Slidell (the Confederate envoy) that the Confederacy might build war-ships in France if 'built as for the Italian government.'" Life of Seward, II, 393, 394.

After Gettysburg and Vicksburg, the South ought to have given up the contest and many of her men were of that opinion. She could have made an honorable peace, coming back into the Union, deprived indeed of slavery but receiving compensation for the slaves [1] and retaining the home rule of her State legislatures.

The North had developed a great general in Grant who was ably supported by Sherman, Sheridan, and Thomas, while the South had suffered the irreparable loss of Stonewall Jackson. With superior resources, with armies larger than those of the

[1] On Feb. 5, 1865, sixty-three days before Lee's surrender, Lincoln recommended that Congress empower the President to pay to the eleven States of the Southern Confederacy, then in arms against the Union, and to the five slave States, remaining in the Union, $400,000,000 in six per cent government bonds as compensation for their slaves, provided that all resistance to the national authority should cease on April 1st. One half should then be paid and the other half when the Thirteenth Amendment abolishing slavery should become valid law. The Cabinet disapproved unanimously of the President's project and it was not submitted to Congress. V, 82. It is hardly likely that Congress would have passed such a bill, as the Southern Confederacy was then tottering. But directly after Gettysburg and Vicksburg, the Cabinet and Congress would undoubtedly have been glad at the cessation of the war, if the Union could have been restored and slavery abolished on the basis of Lincoln's offer.

South, better equipped and supplied and as well disciplined; with generals equal in ability, the North was certain to win in the end, provided she would with persistency and patience make the necessary sacrifice of men and money. Herein Lincoln showed his power for it was he who held the North to its labors. History confirms the contemporaneous impression of John Hay who at twenty-five, the President's private secretary residing in the White House, wrote of Lincoln in his affectionate Western manner: "The old man sits here and wields like a backwoods Jupiter the bolts of war and the machinery of government with a hand equally steady and equally firm." [1]

[1] Private letter to his friend and associate, Nicolay, of Sept. 11, 1863. On Aug. 7, Hay wrote: "The Tycoon [Lincoln] is in fine whack. He is managing this war, the draft, foreign relations, and planning a reconstruction of the union all at once. I never knew with what tyrannous authority he rules the Cabinet till now. The most important things he decides and there is no cavil. I am growing more and more firmly convinced that the good of the country absolutely demands that he should be kept where he is till this thing is over. There is no man in the country so wise, so gentle and so firm. I believe the hand of God placed him where he is." Letters of John Hay, I, 90, 102.

Exercising more authority than any English-
man since Cromwell[1] and achieving success
sufficiently noteworthy to overshadow his
many mistakes, the President had gained
the support not only of the plain people but
also of the business men and of a considerable portion of the independent thought of
the country. He now received in striking
unanimity, the approval of farmers, small
shop-keepers, salesmen, clerks, mechanics,
and men who stood intellectually for lofty
aspirations. " History," wrote James Russell Lowell in 1864, " will rank Lincoln
among the most prudent of statesmen and
the most successful of rulers. If we wish to
appreciate him we have only to conceive
the inevitable chaos in which we should
now be weltering had a weak man or an
unwise one been chosen in his stead."[2]

[1] James Bryce's opinion, IV, 234.

[2] IV, 461. The development of faith in Lincoln, shown in
Charles Eliot Norton's letters to George W. Curtis, is interesting.
On Aug. 24, 1861, he wrote : " If another reverse [after Bull Run]
were to come and they [Cameron, Welles, Smith, members of
Lincoln's Cabinet] still there, the whole Cabinet would have to
go ; — and then let Mr. Lincoln himself look out for a Committee

The brave and high-spirited people of the
South were still determined on resistance;
so the war went on, lasting nearly two
years after Gettysburg and Vicksburg.

In the autumn of 1863 Grant won another important victory in the West. The
President, Congress and the people were
now of one mind regarding the great commander and the President placed him in
command of the armies of the United States.

of Safety." Dec. 5, 1861: "We are very serious over the President's message. We think it very poor in style, manner and
thought — very wanting in pith, and exhibiting a mournful deficiency of strong feeling and wise forecast in the President."
March 8, 1862: "Lincoln's style is worse than ever; and though
a bad style is not always a mark of bad thought, it is at least a
proof that thought is not as clear as it ought to be." Nov. 12,
1862: "The worst of the *ifs* is the one concerning Lincoln. I am
very much afraid that a domestic cat will not answer when one
wants a Bengal tiger." Sept. 3, 1863: Norton spoke of "the extraordinary excellence of the President's letter [letter of Aug. 26.
Complete Works, II, 397]. He rises with each new effort and his
letters are successive victories." Dec. 10, 1863: "Once more we
may rejoice that Abraham Lincoln is President. How wise and
how admirably tuned is his Proclamation [of Dec. 8, 1863 in connection with his annual message of the same date. Complete
Works, II, 442]. As a state paper its naïveté is wonderful. Lincoln will introduce a new style into state papers; he will make
them sincere and his honesty will compel even politicians to like
virtue. I conceive his character to be on the whole the great net
gain from the war." *Atlantic Monthly*, November 1912, 603–612.

Grant saw that his place was with the Army of the Potomac; that he must pit himself against the redoubtable Robert E. Lee. In May 1864, he began his campaign by hurling his troops against the veterans of the Army of Northern Virginia. After two days of fighting, in which he had the worse of the encounter, he gave the order for a night march. His army aware only of a great slaughter started without knowing whether it had been beaten, and when the parting of the ways was reached, the question uppermost in all minds was, Would the orders be to turn northward? But the command, File right, set the men's faces towards Richmond. The soldiers sang and stepped forward with elastic tread. As Grant rode past in the darkness they recognized him and burst into cheers, swung their hats, clapped their hands and threw up their arms greeting their general as a comrade and letting him witness their joy at learning that he was leading them onward to Richmond instead of ordering them to fall back to the camp which they had just abandoned.[1]

Lee found in Grant a very different antagonist from those whom he had so easily overcome. During the battle of the second day his intense anxiety led him to spur forward his horse and follow a Texas brigade that had been ordered to charge home the enemy. He was recognized and from the entire line came the cry "Go back, General Lee! go back!"[2]

For five and forty days Grant prosecuted his campaign of attrition and his loss was enormous. He was bitterly disappointed at the result, as he had failed to crush or capture Lee's army whose power of effective resistance still remained. His own army was shattered and worn out; what remained of it needed rest. To those soldiers must have occurred the thought which ran so many times through the Army of the Potomac: "It is no use. No matter who is given us, we can't whip Bobby Lee."

[1] IV, 440–448.   [2] IV, 441.

Reënforcements and reorganization were indispensable preliminaries to any further offensive operations on a large scale. Grant did not assume a vigorous offensive from June 18, 1864 until the spring of 1865.[1] But his strong will and native hardihood overcame his first disappointment whilst a stolid countenance masked any apprehension he may have had for the future. At the end of this campaign he transferred his army to a point south of Richmond,[2] uncovering Washington, which the Confederates threatened and might have entered, but for the procrastination of Early, the general in command.

In July and August 1864 the North passed through its final period of dejection and misgiving.[3] Lincoln, standing for reëlection feared defeat as a consequence of the failure of Grant's campaign. But a

[1] IV, 440, 488.

[2] This movement, which began June 12, 1864 and ended June 16, was very successfully accomplished.   IV, 488.

[3] Welles made this entry Aug. 17, " I am sadly oppressed with the aspect of things."   Diary, II, 109.

change of fortune was at hand. Farragut
defeated the Confederate fleet and became
master of Mobile Bay, closing an important
port available for blockade running. Here
was another link completed in the chain
that the navy had been steadily forging to
obstruct the intercourse of the Confederacy
with the outside maritime world. Sherman,
after a four months' campaign, in which he
had fought his way south inch by inch, took
Atlanta.[1] If Lincoln's reëlection had ever
been doubtful, these and other victories
made it certain. In November he was
chosen triumphantly for a second presidential term; by their votes the Northern people
declared that the war must be prosecuted
until slavery was destroyed and the Union
restored; and that, to use Lincoln's humor-
ous illustration, "they concluded that it is
not best to swop horses while crossing the

[1] IV, 523, 524. Charles Eliot Norton wrote to George W. Curtis
under date of Sept. 6, 1864 : " And now let us rejoice together over
the great good news. It lifts the cloud and the prospect clears.
We really see now the beginning of the end." *Atlantic Monthly*,
November 1912, 613.

stream." [1]   Before the end of the year, Sherman cut the Southern Confederacy in twain by his famous march to the sea, presenting the city of Savannah to Lincoln as a Christmas gift.[2]

On March 29, 1865, Grant began his final movement against Lee's army. He compelled the evacuation of Richmond and, following in eager pursuit these veterans, led by their great and beloved general, hemmed them in and forced their surrender at Appomattox. In the history of most nations, isolated events are to be found which reveal the principal actors rising suddenly above the common clay to assume heroic size and a sublime demeanor. Such an event was the meeting between Lee and Grant. The one was grieved to the heart;

[1] Lincoln, Complete Works, II, 532, has "river" but a Westerner would surely have said, stream. Appleton's Ann. Cyc., 1864, p. 789 has it, "I am reminded . . . of a story of an old Dutch farmer, who remarked to a companion once that 'it was not best to swop horses when crossing streams.'" Samuel R. Gardiner quotes it "it is not well to swop horses in the middle of a stream." Cromwell's Place in History, 48. My own recollection of the saying is, "it is not well to swop horses while crossing a stream."

[2] IV, 538; V, 29.

the other showed no exultation. As Grant wrote twenty years later when his own death was near, " I felt like anything rather than rejoicing at the downfall of a foe who had fought so long and valiantly." Grant was magnanimous, Lee was appreciative. Generous terms were offered and accepted. When the Union soldiers heard of the surrender they began firing salutes. Grant ordered them stopped, saying, " The war is over; the rebels are our countrymen again." [1]

Meanwhile Sherman had marched northward from Savannah through the Confederacy and, coming up with Johnston commanding the other great Southern army, compelled his surrender. This ended the war. [2]

Between the surrender of Lee and the surrender of Johnston, our country suffered the greatest disaster in its history. Lincoln was assassinated. Of this cruel blow Walt Whitman sang,

[1] V, 129 *et ante*.   [2] V, 166.

"Our fearful trip is done,
The ship has weathered every rack, the prize we sought
    is won,
But our Captain lies fallen cold and dead." [1]

Although exasperated by the assassination of Lincoln the North was at the same

[1] V, 140.   Whitman added:
"O Captain! my Captain! rise up and hear the bells;
Rise up — for you the flag is flung — for you the bugle trills,
For you bouquets and ribbon'd wreaths — for you the shores a-crowding,
For you they call, the swaying mass, their eager faces turning."

LEAVES OF GRASS.

Tom Taylor wrote in *Punch*:

"*You* lay a wreath on murdered Lincoln's bier,
You, who with mocking pencil wont to trace,
    Broad for the self-complacent British sneer,
    His length of shambling limb, his furrowed face,
*   *   *   *   *   *
    Beside this corpse, that bears for winding-sheet
The Stars and Stripes he lived to rear anew,
    Between the mourners at his head and feet,
    Say, scurril jester, is there room for *you?*

Yes, he had lived to shame me from my sneer —
To lame my pencil, and confute my pen —
    To make me own this hind of princes peer,
    This rail-splitter a true-born king of men."

Punch, May 6, 1865. See Layard, Shirley Brooks of *Punch*, 245.

The assassination of Lincoln took place on April 14, 1865.
Under date of April 29, John Bright wrote to Sumner: "For
fifty years I think no other event has created such a sensation in
this country as the great crime which has robbed you of your President.   The whole people positively mourn and it would seem as if
again we were one nation with you, so universal the grief and the
horror at the deed of which Washington has been the scene." —
Pierce's Sumner, IV, 240.

time inspired by the grandeur of Grant's conduct at Appomattox. Nobody was hanged for a political crime, no land of the vanquished Confederates confiscated.[1]

Our civil war lasted four years. And a question often asked is, How was the South able to resist so long? No student of the subject will be inclined to refer their power of protracted resistance to a single cause; nevertheless any one who may live the time over again will find it difficult to escape the conviction that the paramount factor was Robert E. Lee.[2] His ability and character made him the head and center of the Southern cause. When a Southerner had conscientious misgivings, he was reassured by the reflection that any cause winning the devotion of Lee must be just and holy; when he doubted if ultimate success were

[1] " Since their (the Americans') most noble closing of the Civil War, I have looked to them as the hope of our civilization." — George Meredith to W. M. Fullerton, Nov. 15, 1886. *Scribners Magazine*, Sept., 1912, 286.

[2] Under date of May 16, 1865 John Bright wrote to Sumner " For the last two years Lee has been the soul of the whole rebel military action."—Mass. Hist. Soc. Proceedings, XLVI, 139.

possible he remembered that Lee was leading and Lee could not fail. Doubt and
despair were always removed until at Appomattox they penetrated the soul of Lee
himself, when he said, " There is nothing
left me but to go and see General Grant
and I would rather die a thousand deaths."[1]
After the surrender,[2] Lee said to his soldiers
in a suppressed and tremulous voice, " We
have fought through the war together. I
have done the best I could for you. My
heart is too full to say more." [3]

Another and more frequently recurring
question is, How was the North able to
overcome the South ? The opinion of an
intelligent foreign country often foreshadows
the issue of civil strife. Yet in England
friend, foe and neutral alike believed that
the South was not to be subdued. At the
North as at the South one man was the predominant factor in the war. It is true that
some find the determining element of victory
in Grant and Sherman who prevailed over

[1] V, 125.   [2] April 9, 1865.   [3] V, 129.

Lee and Johnston; others find it in the blockade. Yet the affair of supreme difficulty was to get troops for Grant and Sherman, ships and sailors for the blockade. When a democracy goes to war men and money are forthcoming only by voluntary effort; if the people lack confidence in the leader their effort is likely to come to naught. Lincoln possessed this confidence. He was able to give his generals the support they required as well as to supply the means for the blockade; he was unquestionably the one man that the North could not spare.[1]

[1] " The best aspect of an age of controversy must be sought in the lives of the best men, whose honesty carries conviction to the understanding, whilst their zeal kindles the zeal of the many. A study of the lives of such men will lead to the conclusion that, in spite of internecine hostility in act, the real and true leaders had far more in common than they knew of." Stubbs, Constitutional History of England, III, 639.

INDEX

116; troops withdrawn, 117;
restored to command, popu-
larity in army, 118; Antie-
tam campaign, neglected op-
portunity, 119–121; removed,
138.
Madison, James, on slavery, 6.
March to the sea, 190.
Maryland, does not secede, 95.
Mason, J. M., Fugitive Slave
Law, 17, 18; *Trent* affair,
162–166.
Meade, G. G., commands army,
Gettysburg, 146-148.
Mediation, Napoleon's policy,
141, 171; British policy
(1862), abrupt change, 171–
175; England as obstacle to
European offer, 181.
Meredith, George, on closing of
Civil War, 193n.
Merrimac-Monitor fight, 111.
Mexican War, as Southern
war, 11.
Mill, J. S., on Civil War, 2.
Missouri, and slavery in Kansas,
31, 32; does not secede, 95.
Missouri Compromise, 21; re-
peal, 23, 24; Northern con-
demnation of repeal, 26, 28,
30; declared void by Su-
preme Court, 42; suggested
restoration, 71, 74.
Mobile Bay, battle, 189.
Mommsen, Theodor, on slavery
in Rome, 6, 86.
Monitor-Merrimac fight, 111.

Napoleon III, and Civil War,
141, 171, 181.
Nationalism as issue in Civil
War, 5.
Navy, *Merrimac-Monitor* duel,
111; capture of New Orleans,
112; Confederate English-
built vessels, 169, 179; battle
of Mobile Bay, 189.

Nebraska, expected free-state
organization, 31.
Neutrality, British proclamation, 152; *Trent* affair as
violation of right, 161–168;
building of Confederate vessels as violation of duty, 169,
179.
New Mexico, free territory
under Mexican law, 7; Compromise of 1850, 16.
New Orleans, capture, 111.
New York *Tribune*, political
influence, 30.
Norton, C. E., disheartened
(1862), 118n.; on possible
war with England, 167n.;
development of faith in Lincoln, 184n.; on capture of
Atlanta, 189n.
Nullification movement, 3.

Palmerston, Lord, on issues
of Civil War, 154; belief in
Southern success, 156; and
mediation, 171, 172, 174.
Peace Congress, 75.
Peninsular campaign, 113–116;
effect on the North, 116;
withdrawal of troops, 117.
Pickett, G. E., charge at Gettys-
burg, 147.
Pittsburg Landing, battle, 112.
Pope, John, command, 117;
second Bull Run campaign,
118.
Popular sovereignty, doctrine,
25.
Population, greater increase in
North, 10; of North and
South (1860), 95.
Pottawatomie massacre, 35.
Punch, on Lincoln, 192n.

Reconstruction, probable effect of Lincoln's gradual
emancipation policy, 137.

This Index was made for me by David M. Matteson.